AF578071

THE PRACTICE OF NOT REACTING

THE PRACTICE OF NOT REACTING

Zen Wisdom for a Happy Life

RYUSHUN KUSANAGI

PORTFOLIO / PENGUIN

PORTFOLIO / PENGUIN
An imprint of Penguin Random House LLC
1745 Broadway, New York, NY 10019
penguinrandomhouse.com

Most Portfolio books are available at a discount when purchased in quantity for sales promotions or corporate use. Special editions, which include personalized covers, excerpts, and corporate imprints, can be created when purchased in large quantities. For more information, please call (212) 572-2232 or e-mail specialmarkets@penguinrandomhouse.com. Your local bookstore can also assist with discounted bulk purchases using the Penguin Random House corporate Business-to-Business program. For assistance in locating a participating retailer, e-mail B2B@penguinrandomhouse.com.

BOOK DESIGN BY TANYA MAIBORODA

Library of Congress Control Number Permalink: https://lccn.loc.gov/2025055067

ISBN 9798217182381 (hardcover)
ISBN 9798217182398 (ebook)

First published in Japan as HANNO SHINAI RENSHU by KADOKAWA CORPORATION, Tokyo, in 2015.
First English translation published by Rider, an imprint of Penguin Random House Ltd., London, in 2026.
First United States edition published by Portfolio, 2026.
English translation rights arranged with KADOKAWA CORPORATION, Tokyo through Emily Books Agency Ltd., Taipei and Casanovas & Lynch Literary Agency S.L.U., Barcelona.

Printed in the United States of America
1st Printing

The authorized representative in the EU for product safety and compliance is Penguin Random House Ireland, Morrison Chambers, 32 Nassau Street, Dublin D02 YH68, Ireland, https://eu-contact.penguin.ie.

CONTENTS

INTRODUCTION

A Mindset for Solving Life's Frustrations

CHANCES ARE YOU'VE had more than a few moments in life when you've thought, "This just isn't fair," "I can't believe this is happening" or "I just can't deal with this right now."

But what if I told you there's a way to overcome your everyday frustrations?

At the heart of it all, our worries and troubles boil down to a single root cause. Once you grasp that, you'll find that the solution lies in simply shifting your mindset. That's the key lesson I want to share with you in this book.

So, what kinds of frustrations do we face in our daily lives?

- Feeling constantly rushed, with no time to breathe or clear your mind.

- Feeling unsatisfied and anxious about what the future holds.
- Feeling down after a string of bad luck, unpleasant events or failures.
- Struggling with people whose personalities clash with yours.

At first glance, these problems might seem like tough, time-consuming issues—challenges we can't hope to resolve on our own. But here's the surprising truth: they aren't as complicated as they seem.

Why? Because all of these challenges ultimately come down to one thing: reactions of the mind.

It's no exaggeration to say that our daily lives are shaped by how our minds react.

Think about it. On your way to work, you might groan inwardly about the traffic. That moment of frustration can cast a shadow over your whole morning. Perhaps someone cuts you off or pushes past you, and a surge of irritation flares—maybe even anger. Or, before a big presentation, your mind flashes to the worst-case scenario and, suddenly, your chest tightens, your stomach knots. These aren't just passing thoughts—they're emotional reactions that ripple through your body, feeding stress and anxiety.

Whether we're meeting people, engaged in work or simply walking outside, our minds are constantly reacting. As a result, everyday annoyances, disappointments, pressures, regrets, anxieties about the future—they all spiral into overwhelming frustrations.

Behind every problem is a reaction of the mind.

Imagine how much lighter life would feel if you could address the root cause and let go of those reactions. No more getting flustered, feeling down, becoming angry, buckling under pressure, feeling nervous around others, regretting the past or fretting about the future. Just imagine—true relief. You would feel free, and happiness would naturally follow.

People often misunderstand this point, but choosing not to react doesn't mean suppressing your emotions, brushing things off or pretending you don't care. It's about not letting those automatic, knee-jerk, unnecessary reactions take control. It's about hitting the reset button—regaining your peace of mind when emotions like anger, anxiety or that persistent "I'm just not good enough" start to creep in.

How many headaches do we create for ourselves? How many unnecessary messes do we stumble into because of reactions we didn't need to have? Isn't it time to set our sights on a way of life where we let go of those unhelpful reactions and focus on what truly matters? The ancient Indian sage—the Buddha—is here to guide us on exactly that journey.

The Art of Not Reacting

When people face problems, their instinct is to fight back. We go head-to-head with difficult people, frustrating situations and unfair realities. We react, struggle and push hard to change things—to *win*.

But the truth is, most of life's problems aren't things you can win by fighting. No matter how much power, money or influence you gain, reality will always have its own way of unfolding. Struggles and setbacks are woven into our existence—and no one is exempt.

This is the unshakable truth the Buddha pointed out over 2,500 years ago: suffering is an unavoidable part of life. No matter how much you resist, some things simply won't bend to your will.

So, what's the alternative? How about a smarter, more rational way to live?

At their core, the Buddha's teachings are about breaking free from this cycle of suffering and struggle by putting a stop to the mind's unnecessary reactions. His wisdom can be distilled into two key practices:

1. Observing your mind's reactions.
2. Thinking rationally.

When you closely *observe your mind's reactions* and inner workings, the restless noise within naturally begins to settle. This is a simple yet transformative way to relieve stress and reset your mood, and is the foundation for letting go of those things that trigger the mind. Observing the mind's reactions involves practices like mindfulness and insight (*vipassana*) or seated (*samatha* or *zazen*) meditation. We'll take a deeper dive into how all this works in Chapter 1.

Thinking rationally means approaching challenges with logic and a clear purpose. In this book, our goal is simple: to stop unnecessary reactions and avoid adding more feelings of frustration to our lives. To achieve that, we'll focus on five key steps:

- Stop making unnecessary judgments. No matter what happens, don't put yourself down. *(Chapter 2)*
- Free yourself from the pain of negative emotions like stress and worry. *(Chapter 3)*
- Live authentically, free from the crushing pressure of other people's opinions. *(Chapter 4)*
- Let go of the habit of obsessing over winning or losing and measuring yourself against others. *(Chapter 5)*
- Strive for a life that truly satisfies you. *(Chapter 6)*

Each of these universally important ideas will be explored through the lens of the Buddha's teachings. In Pali, the term *Buddha* means "one who has achieved total clarity." It's often translated as the "Awakened One." This focus on addressing life's struggles through the wisdom of early Buddhism—the original teachings the Buddha shared in ancient India over 2,500 years ago—is what sets this book apart. The teachings are filled with timeless insights, and each chapter of this book includes clear translations of the Buddha's profound sayings, offering them in plain language with examples that speak to the kinds of situations we all face in our everyday lives.

Early Buddhism is rich with practical tools for rational thinking that remain as relevant as ever in the modern world—and is very different from the religious ideas many people associate with Buddhism. My hope is that you'll discover how these practical insights can transform your daily life.

There's no need to keep struggling. By following the Buddha's example, we can work toward a life where unnecessary reactions no longer hold us back. No matter what each day brings, we can learn to face our frustrations with clarity and resolve our stresses effectively through clear thinking.

This mindset will lay the foundation for cultivating peace, contentment and true happiness, and is the single most important habit we can develop for a fulfilling life.

—Ryushun Kusanagi

THE PRACTICE OF NOT REACTING

CHAPTER 1

BEFORE REACTING, UNDERSTAND

Don't Try to Eliminate Worries—Understand Them

WE'VE ALL HEARD the saying that life is full of worries. But have you ever stopped to ask yourself, "What exactly *are* my worries?" Surprisingly few people are able to clearly define them.

That vague sense of dissatisfaction, that nagging thought of "Am I really okay with my life the way it is?"—these feelings persist because we don't fully understand what's bothering us. Whether it's frustration at work, conflicts with loved ones or feelings of disappointment, anger or anxiety, we struggle because we lack the right mindset to deal with our emotions. And so, the cycle of dissatisfaction continues.

The Buddha's approach starts by helping us understand the worries we face in our daily lives.

Understanding Your Worries Is the First Step Forward

Life doesn't always go the way we want. Difficult people exist. We all have our own inner weaknesses. But why does any of this end up turning into *suffering*?

Because we only know one way to respond: *reacting*.

We react with anger. We get swept away by desires. We let our thoughts run wild. Before we know it, we're clinging to these emotions, weighed down by them, unable to move forward.

In Buddhism, this state of blindness has long been called *ignorance* (*avijja*)—a mind that simply *doesn't see*. But if you can step back and watch your reactions, if you can understand your worries and catch them in the moment, if you can let them go instead of indulging them, you will free yourself from suffering. Challenges will still come your way, but suffering itself will no longer control you.

This is what the Buddha's wisdom offers—a way to understand your mind correctly, so that you can think in a way that frees you.

Let's take a moment to observe the kinds of thoughts that might run through your mind day to day:

- "My job feels pointless. This isn't how I thought things would turn out."

- "I'm tired of the mess in my relationships. Everything feels like too much."
- "I keep replaying the past. No matter what I do, I can't let it go."
- "I can't say what I really feel. It builds up and eats at me from the inside."
- "I'm anxious all the time. The future feels like a blank wall, and I have no idea where I'm going."

Do any of these sound familiar? On top of these, life throws all sorts of unexpected challenges our way—accidents, illness, family troubles . . . we all have our burdens to carry.

The Buddha categorizes these human struggles into what is called the "Eight Sufferings":

Life itself is suffering.

Aging is suffering.

Illness is suffering.

Death is suffering.

Being forced to interact with people you dislike is suffering.

Being separated from those you love is suffering.

Not getting what you want is suffering.

The constant turmoil of the human mind is suffering.

—"The Buddha's First Sermon," *The Great Chapter*

The Buddha's term for suffering was *dukkha*, an ancient Pali term combining the words *du*, meaning "hardship" or "obstruction," and *kha*, which roughly means an "emptiness that cannot be filled." In essence, *dukkha* is the deep sense of unease, pain and dissatisfaction that runs through our lives—it's the feeling that no matter what we do, something is always missing or just out of reach.

One of the defining features of the Buddha's approach is his willingness to face reality head-on. He starts by acknowledging a simple truth: life comes with struggles. Feeling unfulfilled, burdened or lost? That's part of being human. Instead of denying or avoiding these feelings, the Buddha encourages us to recognize them for what they are, with clarity and honesty.

Now, you might be thinking, "But isn't accepting reality kind of depressing?" Not at all. This isn't about surrendering to misery, it's about seeing things as they are. The Buddha himself went through this shift—he left a life of extraordinary privilege to confront life's harshest truths, discovering that this clarity was anything but bleak. As you will come to see, there's a world of difference between understanding and giving in. The first moves you forward, the second keeps you stuck. When you say, "I have struggles. I have unresolved problems," that isn't defeat—it's awareness. And awareness is the first step toward change.

Most of us go through life feeling vaguely dissatisfied,

weighed down by an unease we can't quite name. That's why the feeling lingers—because we haven't fully acknowledged it. But the moment we do, the moment we say, "Yes, something is missing" or "Yes, I have struggles," we shift from passive suffering to active problem-solving. Understanding what *is*—that's where real transformation begins.

Recognizing that you have feelings of unfulfillment and unresolved stresses isn't a setback—it's the first move toward resolution, and it's the foundation for every step the Buddha's teachings will take us through in this book.

Fortunately, the Buddha left us a roadmap for cultivating exactly this awareness. Let's take a look.

A Clear, Logical Roadmap to Problem-Solving

Once you've acknowledged that you have a problem, the next step is to ask yourself, "What exactly is causing this?"

The Buddha laid out a straightforward, four-step approach to dealing with suffering:

> *Life inevitably comes with suffering.*
>
> *Every kind of suffering has a cause.*
>
> *That suffering can be eliminated.*
>
> *There is a method to eliminate it.*
>
> —"The Buddha's First Teaching at Sarnath," *The Connected Discourses*

In Buddhism, these are known as the "Four Noble Truths." They may seem self-evident, but that's the point. Buddhism isn't a religion of faith or blind belief. It never says, "Believe in this, and you'll be saved." Buddhism instead encourages you to think in a way that allows you to break free from suffering. In other words, it's a mindset shift in how you relate to life—one that can lead to real peace.

The Buddha's method is much like the approach a doctor takes. First, you identify the problem: worries exist. Then, you examine its root cause: every worry has a root cause. Finally, you follow a treatment plan to relieve the symptoms and restore balance: worries can be resolved. There's nothing abstract or mystical about it. It's a clear, step-by-step process for understanding the nature of suffering and finding a path out of it. Like good medicine, it's based on careful observation and experience—not faith or dogma.

By breaking it down this way, the Buddha offers a powerful, rational way to overcome any problem. That is the central theme of this book and is a method we'll explore in detail as we work through the chapters to come. First, let's look at exactly what *is* the root cause of suffering.

What Really Lies Behind Your Work and Relationship Problems?

Buddhism often points to *attachment*—our inability to let go. Attachment means clinging to things, getting stuck on desires, regrets, anger or fears. We hold on to things so tightly that we end up making ourselves miserable.

Why is it so hard to let go of our worries and attachments? Why do we keep getting caught up in so many problems, big and small? As we touched on in the introduction, it all comes down to one thing: our mind's automatic reactions.

In our daily lives, we are constantly reacting, continually thinking about something. We get annoyed when things don't go our way. We feel anxious about what others might think of us. We stew over past mistakes, wondering if we did something wrong. All of these are examples of the mind reacting to our experiences.

And what do these reactions lead to? We lash out in anger and damage relationships. We choke under pressure and fail to perform at our best. We replay painful memories and sink into regret. We overthink everything and convince ourselves that we're not good enough.

Ultimately, these habits of thought are what drive our suffering. The root cause isn't attachment itself—it's your mind's reactions.

You might be nodding along right now, thinking, "That's

exactly it. I'm constantly reacting to everything around me. And when my reactions don't go the way I want, I end up frustrated." That's because your reactions are the true culprit behind your suffering. It's your mind's reflexive responses that trigger stress, anxiety and all the troubles you face in life.

So, if there's one thing we need to start practicing every day, it's this: not to fight or suppress our reactions, but to notice them clearly. The first step isn't to eliminate them overnight, but to become aware of how they arise and what they do to us. This simple act of observation creates the space for a calmer, more intentional response. Only then can we truly stop wasting energy on those unnecessary reactions and start thinking rationally.

The Real Reason Behind Your Struggles

We've already uncovered a crucial truth: that all suffering begins with your mind's reactions. But now, you need to ask, "Why do I react the way I do?" That question lies at the heart of this book's purpose—to help you see your mind clearly, understand its patterns and free yourself from the suffering they create.

If something bad happens and you get angry, the reason behind that reaction seems obvious—the bad thing itself.

But life isn't always that simple. Sometimes, we react in ways that don't make sense, even to ourselves. Have you ever found yourself feeling irritated, stressed or anxious without fully understanding why? Some people try to find answers through things like therapy or counseling. While those methods can help, the Buddha's wisdom provides an instant shortcut to clarity. Let's say you've been feeling increasingly frustrated with people lately. Maybe your family has always annoyed you, but now you're finding yourself irritated by coworkers and friends, even random strangers. Everything they do gets under your skin and, honestly, it's exhausting.

So, you turn to others for advice. And here's what they tell you:

"You should try to relax."

"Don't take it personally."

"You're expecting too much from everyone—just focus on the good stuff."

Sure, they make good points, but, somehow, their words don't really help. You go back to your daily life and, soon enough, that familiar irritation creeps back in. What's really going on? Why does this frustration keep coming back?

Life as a raging current: The Buddha's take on reality

The Buddha had a profound insight into why people feel dissatisfied or unfulfilled. He put it this way:

Understand why suffering arises.

The source of suffering is the never-ending craving for pleasure.

—"The First Turning of the Wheel,"
The Connected Discourses

Even when our struggles are vague and hard to define, they often share the same root. The Buddha's insight was that behind every form of dissatisfaction lies a deeply ingrained craving (*tanha*)—the constant energy of our mind's reactive tendencies. Craving is an underlying current that runs through us all our lives, shaping how we think, feel and act.

This craving branches out into seven core desires:

1. Survival instinct (the desire to stay alive)
2. Sleep (the desire to rest)
3. Hunger (the desire to eat)
4. Libido (the desire for intimacy)
5. Laziness (the desire to avoid effort)
6. Sensory pleasure (the desire for comfortable surroundings and novel experiences)
7. The need for recognition (the desire to be acknowledged)

These seven desires exist in all of us, which means we can break down human life into the following cycle:

1. There is a craving.
2. That craving gives rise to the seven desires.
3. We react based on those desires.
4. Sometimes, we feel joy when our desires are satisfied. Other times, we feel frustrated when they aren't.
5. This cycle repeats endlessly.

The Buddha compared this turbulent cycle of joy, sorrow, frustration and longing to the powerful, overflowing rivers of India. He called it the *raging current* of human existence.

Sound familiar? It's a pretty accurate description of modern life, too.

> *Craving fuels the endless cycle of suffering—an unquenchable thirst that keeps us trapped.*
>
> *These countless desires push and pull at us like a raging current.*
>
> *Humans find themselves drowning in the muddy waters of their own unchecked wants.*
>
> —"The Struggle," *The Collection of Discourses*

How Do We Make Peace with an Unfulfilled Heart?

In Buddhist teachings, this craving is often referred to as *thirsting desire*—a mind that is always wanting, always unsatisfied. That describes the human experience pretty well, doesn't it?

The important thing to understand is that this is just how the mind works. It's wired to crave. And because it craves, it's never fully content. If we don't recognize this, we fall into the trap of blindly following these cravings. We chase novelty, thinking that, this time, we'll feel fulfilled. We reminisce about the past, telling ourselves, "Life was better back then." We get frustrated with our work, jumping from job to job. We might end up seeking intense thrills—affairs, drugs, risky behavior—trying to fill the void. Or we might inflate our egos, telling ourselves, "I deserve better than this."

Of course, seeking something better isn't necessarily wrong, but the Buddha's point was this: "Even when we get what we want, it doesn't guarantee satisfaction. The mind always wants more." Reacting to our cravings is often just a waste of energy and leads to an unfulfilled heart.

Some people might think, "If that's how it is, what's the point?" But here's the fascinating part—when you fully accept that the mind is wired to crave, something shifts inside you. That nagging sense of emptiness, that restless need for *more*, starts to settle down. You stop seeing it as a personal flaw or an urgent problem to fix. Instead, you start seeing your desire for what it is—and, in that acceptance, there's a kind of peace. We'll be diving deeper into acceptance in the final chapter.

Our Desire for Recognition

Let's go back to that earlier frustration—feeling dissatisfied with the people around you. Where does that feeling really come from? If we trace it back to the seven desires, we often find it's rooted in one specific craving, which is perhaps the most pressing theme for us in modern times: the need for recognition. This desire to be acknowledged, to be validated, is entirely unique to humans. Animals don't care about social status, but we certainly do.

As children, this desire starts with wanting love and approval from our parents. As we move into our teens, it often becomes about getting good grades, being popular, being told we're doing well—anything that makes us feel like we matter. When we reach adulthood, this desire can manifest itself as a drive for career promotions, seeking jobs or positions that command respect or honing our skills for advancement. On the flip side, it also fuels pride ("I want to be seen as better than others"), guilt ("I feel like I'm not good enough"), envy ("Why do they have what I don't?") and a constant urge to compare ourselves to others ("I'm a failure").

What drives these feelings is the desire for validation—wanting to be acknowledged, to be loved, to be appreciated. When these needs dictate how we react to the outside world, we often feel like no one around us is meeting our expectations, which leads to dissatisfaction and a sense of unfulfillment.

We get frustrated, feeling like people and the world just aren't measuring up to our desire for recognition.

So, what's really behind that constant frustration with the little things people do? It's often just this: "I wish they would acknowledge me more."

As we've seen, the first step in overcoming this frustration is to return to the Buddha's teachings and start with a simple but essential practice: understand.

Try saying this:

"This frustration is really just my craving for recognition."

"This dissatisfaction is merely my unmet desire to be acknowledged."

You can even rephrase it—recognition-seeking, desire, attachment. Use whichever term resonates with you. The key is to say it, think it and process it objectively.

When you do this, your emotional reactions will begin to quiet down.

In later chapters, we'll explore how this same need for recognition fuels a range of different problems we might face, including being overly concerned with other people's opinions, feeling envious all the time and fixating on comparisons, superiority and winning or losing against other people.

If we don't acknowledge our need for recognition, we get sucked into endless comparison games. We care too much about what other people think. We let envy eat away at us. We keep competing, always chasing the next win. We feel high when we're ahead and crushed when we fall behind. The result is a cycle of constant emotional turmoil.

And so, the first step is simply to understand what's happening.

What if, instead of fighting it, you simply admitted it to yourself? It can be surprisingly liberating: "I have a deep need for recognition."

It's odd how simply acknowledging this can ease so much dissatisfaction—the frustrations, the feelings of inadequacy, the loneliness that weighed you down. Once you understand that the cause of your heart's craving is this desire for recognition, you can find yourself breaking free from that state of discontent.

And then, a new thought emerges, one that's almost freeing in its simplicity: "Even if they *do* recognize me, so what?"

Because really, does it actually change anything?

A real-life example: The day suffering turned into hope

When you don't understand the real reason behind your struggles, the suffering never seems to end. But once you grasp the true cause, what once felt like a hopeless battle becomes a challenge you can overcome—one that holds the promise of change.

Let me share with you an inspiring story of someone who turned a life of pain into one filled with hope.

When I first met this inspirational woman, she was in her late seventies. For years, she had lived with her eldest son who was in his forties, but, as his violent outbursts escalated, things took a devastating turn—he threw her out of the house, locking the doors behind her. She couldn't get back in, and she had nowhere else to turn.

Just like that, in the final years of her life, she found herself homeless.

Fortunately, she was able to secure welfare support and move into a small apartment. I visited her one scorching summer afternoon, and the first thing she said to me was chilling: "If I don't find a solution today, I'm going to hang myself right here in this room."

She started talking, slowly unraveling the path that had led her to this moment. And as she spoke, one thing became clear—she had been carrying a lifetime of resentment toward her own mother.

Out of her seven siblings, she was the only one who wasn't allowed to attend school. Instead, she was forced to stay home and take care of the household. Even after getting married and having two children of her own, she wasn't given the chance to raise them. "Your job is to take care of the household," her mother reminded her, sending her children away to live with relatives. As a result, she had no memories of their childhood and, for years, they kept telling her that they didn't think of her as their mother.

Her earliest memory of her mother was from when she was hospitalized at six years of age. She remembered sitting by the window, waiting for her mother to visit. And then, she saw her. Her mother walked right past the hospital. She didn't stop. She didn't even turn to look.

"Why won't she come see me?"

That was how she described her first memory of her mother.

Sitting in front of me, she had the delicate, refined features of an elegant woman. You wouldn't think she carried such deep pain. But for decades, she had struggled with the emotional distance between herself and her children, as well as the growing violence of her son. More than anything, she couldn't understand why her life had turned out this way.

Yet, in that moment, she realized why she had always felt so distant from her own children. Even after all these years, her heart was still looking toward her mother. Beneath everything—beneath her pain, her loneliness, her sense of never being enough—she had spent her entire life searching for her mother's love, searching for recognition.

By then, the room had grown dark.

She looked at me and said, "Do you think I can overcome this?"

"Yes," I told her. "You absolutely can."

"What should I do?" she asked.

"Understand," I said. "True understanding is the greatest wisdom there is. Today, you finally uncovered the real reason behind your suffering. From here, all you need to do is keep watching. Pay attention to your thoughts, your emotions, your past. Let them reveal themselves to you, little by little. And, above all, trust in the future."

That was when she made her decision.

"I understand," she said firmly. "From now on, I'll make an effort to truly understand my heart. And I'll make overcoming this pain my life's goal."

When she turned on the light, something had changed. She was no longer the woman who had greeted me with despair in her voice. Her eyes shone with new energy. In that moment, she had freed herself from suffering.

I felt as if I had just witnessed someone becoming enlightened.

A few days later, she took her first step forward.

Instead of focusing on what she had lost, she decided to give back. She went to a local nursing home—not to live there, but to volunteer. She wanted to help care for the elderly, to offer kindness and support. She wanted to put into practice the very thing the Buddha had taught: compassion, and a heart that genuinely wishes for the happiness of others.

There, she struck up a conversation with an older man who maintained the gardens in a local park. She asked if she could help, and he welcomed her. Before long, she had befriended a group of local preschoolers, and they all started working together, clearing grass and tending to the plants.

Even now, she calls me from time to time, always with the same cheerful report: "This is the happiest I've ever been."

If there's such a thing as rebirth or reincarnation, I believe it means transforming a life filled with suffering into one brimming with hope. The key to making that transformation possible is the ability to understand our troubles correctly.

> *We must learn to truly understand the nature of our suffering.*
>
> *We must cut off suffering at its root.*
>
> *We must reach a place where suffering no longer controls us.*
>
> *And we must put into practice the methods that lead us there.*
>
> *I have reached an unshakable conviction—once you grasp this truth, you will never be trapped by suffering again.*
>
> —"The Buddha's First Sermon," *The Great Chapter*

How to Observe Your Mind

We've seen that by developing the habit of observing your mind's workings, you can reduce unnecessary emotional reactions—stress, anger, frustration, anxiety—before they take over.

But what does it actually mean to observe your mind?

Let's break it down into three simple techniques:

1. Label your emotions with words.
2. Tune in to your physical sensations.
3. Categorize what you're feeling.

Each of these is rooted in mindfulness and meditation and has a remarkable calming effect. I've covered each of them in depth below and encourage you to give them a try.

Label your emotions with words

This technique is simple: you acknowledge your emotional state in words. For example, if you feel nervous around someone you dislike, say to yourself, "I feel nervous." If you realize you've spent too much time scrolling through your phone or watching TV, take a moment to say, "My mind feels scattered" or "I feel restless." For an even greater sense of calm, try closing your eyes as you do this.

Throughout the day, ask yourself, "How is my mind feeling right now?" Whether you're at work, with family or alone, take a moment to check in, noting things like, "I feel tired," "My energy is low," "I'm feeling irritable" or "I can't seem to gather my thoughts."

In Buddhist teachings, this technique is sometimes called *labeling*—as if you're sticking a mental name tag on your emotions. By identifying them like this, you create a sense of distance from them, allowing you to comprehend them objectively.

You can also apply labeling to your daily actions. When cleaning, think, "I am cleaning." When washing dishes, think, "I am washing dishes." When walking, think, "I am walking."

When working on your computer, think, "I am working." Just state your actions as you do them.

By making a habit of labeling both your emotions and your actions, you train yourself to observe, rather than react. After a while, here's what you'll start to notice—once you name an emotion, you're no longer trapped by it. The moment you step out of automatic reaction mode, your mind regains its balance.

Labeling emotions isn't just an exercise in mindfulness—it's a fundamental tool for mental well-being.

Tune in to your physical sensations

The second method is focusing on physical sensations. This is an incredibly effective way to refresh your mind and release fatigue and stress.

Try this exercise. Close your eyes and focus on your hands. Notice the subtle sensation of your hands even in the darkness behind your eyelids. Raise your hand slowly. Feel the movement. Acknowledge it: "I feel my hand moving." Bring your hand back down. Keep your awareness on the sensation.

Next, try this. Place your hands on your lap, palms facing up. Slowly clench and unclench your hands. Observe the sensations—"This is what it feels like to close my hand." "This is what it feels like to open my hand." Take some time to do this well.

Now, stand up. As you do, stay aware of the sensations in your body. When you start walking, pay attention to how your feet move, how the soles of your feet press into the floor.

The more you practice this, the more you'll understand what it means to be aware of your body.

Apply the same approach to your breath. Feel your chest expanding and contracting as you breathe. Notice the air moving in and out of your nose.

The key is to pay attention—to *feel* your body instead of just using it on autopilot.

These first two techniques—labeling with words and tuning in to your physical sensations—were known in the Buddha's time as *sati*. In the Zen tradition, it's called *nen*, and in modern meditation practices, we call it mindfulness.

Simply put, it's about being fully aware of your mental state. When you do this, unnecessary emotional reactions fade, your mind settles and you gain a deep sense of focus and inner peace.

Categorize what you're feeling

This final technique involves sorting your mental state into clear categories. It's similar to labeling with words, but instead of naming each feeling precisely, you step back and view your thoughts in broader, more conceptual terms. The three basic categories are *greed*, *anger* and *delusion*.

Greed is the state of being driven by excessive wants and expectations. In short, it's wanting or expecting too much. Feelings of frustration, impatience or dissatisfaction in relationships often stem from this constant need for more.

It's important to regularly ask, "Am I demanding too much from myself?" "Am I expecting too much from others?"

When greed takes control, not only do we make ourselves miserable, we also create suffering for those around us.

> *A person consumed by endless cravings is like a boat with a hole in it—sinking under the weight of its own unchecked desires.*
>
> —"Desire," *The Collection of Discourses*

Anger is what we feel when things don't go our way—when we're irritated, frustrated or stressed. Instead of being swept up by these emotions, recognize them for what they are: "This is anger."

At its core, anger is rooted in desire. We want things a certain way and, when reality doesn't match our expectations, we get upset.

Many people walk through life with a vague sense of dissatisfaction without even realizing why. But constantly feeling annoyed, impatient or frustrated isn't a recipe for happiness.

So, the next time anger arises, remind yourself—"I feel angry right now, but this anger is just a by-product of my own expectations. It may not be as real or as justified as it seems."

This shift in perspective is eye-opening.

That said, if your anger is deeply ingrained, you need to be extra mindful. Some common signs of unresolved anger include:

- having a short temper
- holding on to sadness or grief (yes, sadness is ultimately a form of anger)
- feeling stuck in regret, disappointment or past failures
- carrying self-doubt or a sense of inferiority

Leaving anger unchecked is a waste. Why? Because anger isn't something you have to live with—it's something you can understand and let go of.

If ignored, anger accumulates over time, showing up as chronic irritability, frustration or an all-around difficult personality. The older you get, the more it seeps into your actions, words and even your facial expressions.

Whenever you notice anger within you, don't suppress it—acknowledge it. Simply saying "I feel angry" helps to release it. Over time, this process lightens your heart and clears your mind.

Those who stay mindful and composed do not let anger take control of their words, actions or thoughts. In doing so, they protect their own inner freedom.

—"Anger," ***The Path of the Dhamma***

Delusion (*moha*), in Buddhist teachings, is the state of being caught in unhelpful patterns of thought such as overthinking, worrying about the future or dwelling on the past. As a technical Buddhist term, delusion doesn't mean mental illness. Rather, it refers to the everyday fog that keeps us from seeing things as they really are. Many of our struggles come from this place—"I can't switch my mind off" or "I feel all over the place."

RESETTING THE MIND

So, how do we deal with this tendency to overthink?

The truth is that delusion, in the Buddhist sense, is the most persistent mental affliction we have. Humans are wired to be constantly thinking. If it were only pleasant daydreams, there would be no harm. But, more often than not, we get caught up in worries about work or household chores ("I have so much to do!"), we suddenly feel overwhelmed by anxiety about the future ("What if everything falls apart?") or we dwell on past regrets, sinking into depression ("If only I'd done things differently").

All of this comes from unchecked mental chatter. The key is learning how to reset it.

The first step to stopping unhelpful thoughts is to recognize them in real time. This is what we previously referred to as *labeling*, and it's emphasized in a wide range of Buddhist meditation texts.

Sounds simple, right? But, in practice, it can be surprisingly difficult. That's because we get caught up in thoughts without even realizing it. Most of the time, we only notice after we've already been swept away. Even monks who dedicate their lives to meditation struggle with this.

So, here's a fresh approach, a technique that hasn't been widely talked about before—learn to distinguish between a *delusional state* and a *non-delusional state*.

Try this:

- Close your eyes. Picture anything—what you had for breakfast, a scene from a TV show, anything at all.
- Now, open your eyes and look at the room around you. Observe the details.
- Tell yourself this: "What I was just seeing in my mind, that was a thought. What I see now, this is real, this is my vision at work."

In that moment, the images that had been occupying your mind a moment ago will no longer exist, and you'll have successfully separated imagination from reality.

It's important to be able to distinguish between delusion

and other states. Think of it as delusion versus sight, and delusion versus bodily sensations.

Next, shift your focus to a different kind of bodily sensation, one distinct from your daydreaming. Pay attention to the feeling of the air entering and leaving your nostrils as you breathe, or the sensation of your chest expanding and contracting.

By practicing this, you'll sharpen your ability to recognize thoughts as thoughts, and you'll get better at breaking free from mental traps.

THE PRACTICE OF WALKING TO CLEAR YOUR MIND

You can also use your journey to and from work, or a simple stroll down the street, to clear your mind.

Mentally note, "right, left, right, left" as you walk, feeling the pressure of each step. If you're on a train or other mode of transportation, focus on your breath using words like "inhale, exhale," keeping in sync with the subtle rise and fall of your chest.

Worries always arise from within the mind. As such, the best way to overcome those worries is to shift your focus to the bodily sensations that exist outside of your mind.

This is the opposite of mindlessly scrolling on your phone while walking or traveling, which only reinforces the habit of reacting automatically. When we get too used to quick, half-hearted reactions, our minds become cluttered and restless, and we increase the odds that feelings of emptiness and distraction will manage to creep in.

If you want to reduce stress and increase your sense of fulfillment with life, cut back on reactive thinking and strengthen your awareness of the present moment. To do this, make it a habit to pay attention to your body's sensations.

Try this practice for a few months. You'll likely notice you have a sharper, clearer mind—and a lighter, more peaceful heart.

Once you understand how to focus on your body's sensations as a way of grounding yourself in direct perception rather than getting caught up in thoughts, you can apply this technique anywhere—whether it's sports, yoga, hiking or even simple cardio routines.

Your Secret Tool to Break Free from Reacting

Now, let's take a step back. Buddhism teaches that our emotional reactions form chains. This principle, traditionally known as *dependent origination* (*paticcasamuppada*), can be understood like this:

> *When we lack awareness or understanding, our minds react. A stimulus triggers a reaction, and from that reaction, emotions, desires and delusions start to form. We cling to*

these thoughts, giving rise to particular mental states. Those states, in turn, fuel new reactions, setting off a chain that leads to various forms of suffering.

—**"On the Sequential Unfolding of Dependent Origination,"** ***The Inspired Utterances***

In simple terms, it goes like this:

1. We encounter a stimulus.
2. We react to it.
3. That reaction generates strong emotional energy—feelings, desires, memories or delusions. These are what we call *mental formations* (*sankhara*), strong reactions that stick in our memory and show up in facial expressions and actions.
4. This reaction-based mental formation latches on to a new stimulus and repeats the cycle.

For example, let's say you had a bad experience at work or school. You come home, and that lingering anger makes you snap at your family over something trivial. Maybe you've faced a painful failure deeper in your past, and the old, unresolved anger stays buried—only to flare up later and cause you to lash out. Even past experiences of being bullied can leave an imprint, making you anxious in social settings today. These reactions all stem from unresolved mental formations.

These unresolved reactions function like emotional landmines, which get triggered when we encounter particular situations. Many traits that cause us to label ourselves as "short-tempered," "overly sensitive," "prone to depression" or even "socially anxious" can actually stem from these deeply ingrained reactions.

Recognizing these reactions is crucial. While counseling and medication can help calm the mind, if the root cause is an unresolved mental formation, those solutions alone might not be enough.

A more effective approach is to understand the mental process that led to your current state and to pay attention to the chain of emotions behind a single reaction. Instead of simply reacting, start observing. Realize when you still have lingering anger from the past. Once you become aware of past emotional formations, their hold on you will gradually weaken.

What's the big takeaway from all of this?

To sum up the Buddha's teachings we've discussed so far, the key to mental clarity is to understand before reacting.

- The root of our troubles lies in knee-jerk mental reactions.
- These reactions are craving and the seven desires that arise from it, particularly the desire for recognition.
- To better understand your state of mind, label your emotions with words, shift your focus to your bodily sensa-

tions and categorize your feelings as either greed, anger or delusion.

By training yourself in this, you can start to dismantle unnecessary suffering at its root.

The reason people struggle to break the cycle of overreacting is because they don't see their own minds clearly.

Imagine feeling weighed down by a vague sense of unease. If you don't have a method for recognizing what's causing it, you stay stuck. But if you stop and examine your emotions, asking "What is this driven by?" you might notice, for example, "I'm feeling greedy," "I'm experiencing anger" or "This is just a delusion." Often, you might find that all three are at play.

That alone can be enough to start clearing the fog you're feeling. What you're practicing in that moment is the essence of Buddhism—training to purify the heart.

Traditionally, greed, anger and delusion have been called the "Three Poisons" in Buddhism, and they are considered the three primary human afflictions. Modern interpretations often treat them as negative traits to be suppressed. In the Buddha's time, however, these were actually tools for self-understanding.

Even if you have no interest in Buddhism, here's something that applies to everyone: seeing clearly doesn't mean believing you're right. Trying to impose your own perspective on the world only clouds your perception.

True clarity means stepping outside your own opinions and judgments. It means seeing what *is*—objectively, neutrally and without emotional interference.

When you see clearly, you don't react impulsively. You don't get rattled. You don't dwell on your own thoughts. You simply observe—with a calm, neutral mind. That's what real understanding is, and that's the path to overcoming suffering.

In Buddhist teachings, the state reached by the Buddha, who attained the ultimate level of understanding, is called *emancipation* (*vimutti*), sometimes translated as *liberation* or *release*.

In the end, Buddhism isn't about following a religion. It's about something profoundly practical—gaining freedom from unnecessary mental suffering through clear understanding. This is what lies at the heart of the practice of not reacting.

Try it. See what happens. You might just discover a way of living that makes you say, "This is enough. This is good."

Desire is what brings people to suffering.

Therefore, let go of desire by stepping onto the right path.

And be careful not to fall back into its grip, only to return to a life of suffering.

—**"The Path to the Way Beyond,"**
The Collection of Discourses

Once you've mastered real understanding, the noise within begins to quiet and you can reclaim a sense of ease and start letting go of the things that are weighing you down. You'll then be ready to dive into the first step in thinking rationally: stop making unnecessary judgments.

CHAPTER 2

STOP JUDGING WHAT'S GOOD AND BAD

Are You Making Unnecessary Judgments?

ONE BIG REASON people get stuck in worry and stress is that they overanalyze and judge everything. Judgment fuels our mind's constant reactions—it's the mental habit of immediately labeling experiences as "good" or "bad," "right" or "wrong." This reactive mindset keeps us trapped in cycles of frustration and anxiety.

Judgment means making snap decisions about important things, like whether your work is meaningful or not, whether life is worth living or whether you're better or worse than someone else. It's the mindset that says "I'm worthless" or reacts with "I failed," "I'm screwed" or "I have the worst luck." Anxiety, hesitation, our negative opinions of others—all of these stem from judgments.

Such judgments create endless frustration, gloom and

worry for ourselves. By learning to recognize and control these judgments, we interrupt the automatic chain reaction they trigger in our minds, which, in turn, creates the space needed to practice not reacting.

Imagine how much lighter your mind would feel if you could avoid making unnecessary judgments. Imagine how much more smoothly life could flow. Let's explore that possibility.

Stop Thinking in Terms of "Good" or "Bad" and "Like" or "Dislike"

Take a moment to reflect on just how much judgment controls your thoughts.

For instance, some people are obsessed with trying to predict the future, constantly deciding whether their luck is good or bad. Some thrive on gossip, always analyzing people's actions or beliefs. Others immediately categorize everyone they meet as either good or bad, as someone they like or someone they don't.

Then there are those who always believe *they* are right. They refuse to listen to others, stubbornly pushing their own opinions. Some even lash out when challenged. Sound familiar? A parent, a boss or that one frustrating friend, perhaps?

Judgment also affects your personality. Rigid insistence that things must be a certain way leads to perfectionism, obsessive behavior and overworking. On the flip side, judgments like dismissing yourself as a failure create self-doubt and low self-esteem.

How many times have you told yourself "I'm bound to fail" or "I don't have what it takes," without even trying? These, too, are judgments. Looked at this way, it's easy to see how judgments can control our lives.

> *The awakened do not cling to human opinions, beliefs or rules.*
>
> *They do not judge what is good or bad, nor do they allow judgment to stain their hearts. They do not create the causes of inner turmoil.*
>
> *The Buddha teaches only the right path. And in doing so, he remains free from the ego of I am.*
>
> —"On the Purity of the Heart," *The Collection of Discourses*

The Pleasure of Pretending to Understand

The truth is that everyone has a tendency to judge too much. Why do people feel the need to judge everything—themselves, others, even the meaning of life?

One reason is that *judging feels good.* Deciding what's right or wrong gives you the illusion of understanding. It feels like you've reached a conclusion, which brings a sense of relief.

(Perhaps this ultimately traces back to ancient survival instincts—figuring out "There is food here" or "That place is dangerous.")

Another reason is that *judging makes us feel validated*. After an argument, you might replay the situation in your head, thinking, "That person was wrong" or "They caused this mess." You might even call a friend to vent, hoping to hear them say, "Yeah, you were totally right." That little stamp of approval boosts your ego. You're essentially searching for a judgment that satisfies your desire for recognition-seeking.

In short, judgment brings two types of pleasure: the satisfaction of feeling like you understand and the validation of believing you are right.

That's why people get addicted to making judgments.

If you ever meet someone who seems arrogant, try to see what's really happening inside them. Their judgments come from the fleeting pleasure of feeling right and the deep need to be acknowledged. They're thirsty for validation. And, deep down, they're suffering.

When Judgment Becomes Poison

Judgments might feel good, but when you cling to them too tightly, either you or someone else is bound to suffer for it.

A mother once came to me with a question: "My daughter refuses to study. How can I get her to take her education seriously?"

Digging deeper, I learned that she had enrolled her daughter in an elite, high-pressure private school designed to push students toward acceptance into a top university. The school enforced a brutal study regimen: late-night self-study sessions, strict ranking systems and even changes to school trips based on test scores.

The mother claimed, "I just want her to have a good life." But, in reality, her obsession stemmed from her own resentment. She had failed her own university entrance exams, and now she was trying to live out her lost dream through her daughter.

To the girl, her mother was an unpredictable force—snapping at her over the smallest of mistakes, hurling contradictory comments like, "You'll never get in anyway!" only to subsequently break down in tears, drinking late into the night. For her daughter, it was baffling—she couldn't understand why she was being treated this way or why she was being pushed so hard. Eventually, she began questioning everything—why she was in this family, what the point of her life was. It wasn't long before she started to feel more and more emotionally unstable. One autumn night in her second year of high school, she attempted to take her own life.

Thankfully, she survived. But even after the incident, her mother didn't change. She still pressured her daughter to study, still lashed out with harsh remarks. In fact, she came to me with her question—"How do I get her to study?"—*after* her daughter's suicide attempt.

The girl never harmed herself again, but she eventually dropped out of secondary school without going to university.

This story is heartbreaking, but it's not uncommon. Many people have experienced something similar growing up. Perhaps you, too, may unknowingly be doing the same thing to your own children.

What can we do to recognize this pattern before it's too late?

A Mind That Flows Like a Stream

Buddhism teaches that suffering must be seen for what it is.

Even in this mother's case, the goal isn't to immediately label her as wrong. Instead, we must ask: What caused her suffering? What could help her let go of it?

Her pain came from the thought, "I didn't get into that university." Whether or not one gets into university is a fact of life, but she took it a step further, judging herself for it. "I failed, therefore I'm worthless." It was this judgment that fueled her suffering. That suffering then turned into anger—at herself, at her daughter and at the world. It caused her to lash out, to control, to demand. The more she clung to her unfulfilled dream, the more she and her daughter suffered.

There are three kinds of attachments that create suffering: clinging to what we want but cannot have; clinging to what we have, hoping it will never change, though it will inevitably be lost; and clinging to the desire to eliminate the things that bring us pain, even when they cannot be erased.

True peace comes not from changing reality, but from letting go of these attachments.

—"The Buddha's First Teaching at Sarnath,"
The Connected Discourses

As we touched on in the previous chapter, whenever there is suffering, there is an underlying attachment.

A healthy mind should be like a flowing stream—always moving, never stuck. But attachment creates stagnation, and that's where suffering takes root.

If you or someone close to you is suffering, something is out of balance. Let that suffering be your wake-up call.

As an example, let's break down the mother and daughter's situation through the lens of Buddhist wisdom:

- The mother's unfulfilled dream from the past was creating suffering.
- The thought—"I failed" (or "This wasn't supposed to happen")—was creating suffering.
- The expectation—"My daughter should be like this"—was creating suffering.

If we don't release these attachments, both we and the people around us will continue to suffer.

Don't Mistake What Isn't for What Is

Judgment—rigid assumptions, unrealistic expectations or harsh self-criticism—is just another form of attachment. You could even call it a mental illness.

Such judgments didn't originally have a place in your mind. You probably picked them up from your parents, your teachers, your friends or the endless flood of information that abounds out there in the world.

Of course, some judgments are necessary for decision-making, to work, to live, to plan for the future. Often, decisions can help improve our mental outlook. However, once we become attached to those decisions, to those judgments, that's when suffering begins—because reality is impermanent, constantly changing.

A past dream that didn't come to life is no longer a dream—it's a memory. In the context of the Three Poisons that we met in Chapter 1 (greed, anger and delusion), it's a delusion. If it still feels real, it's because you're holding on to it so tightly. But the truth is, it doesn't exist anymore.

Expectations about how your life or someone else's should be are likewise judgments. And since they exist only in your mind, they, too, are delusions.

This may come as a surprise to many, but it's the truth.

The harsh reality is that holding on to judgments that have become no more than our own delusions brings pain to ourselves and others.

Isn't it time to let them go?

In Buddhism, this mistaken belief—thinking something exists when it actually doesn't—is called *misapprehension* (*vipallasa*).

If a judgment is causing pain, it's a misapprehension.

The only cure for misapprehension is to let go.

A Way to Let Go of Suffering

When you follow the Buddha's example, letting go of judgment can be surprisingly simple. Instead of holding on to ideas about how things *should* be, focus on reality as it is.

Once you understand that judgment exists only in your mind, once you realize, "Wait a minute—judgment is just a mental illusion. That's it?," it's like discovering you've been scared of a shadow all your life. The moment you truly see reality, the darkness lifts and, from there, you can build a life where both you and those around you can truly be happy.

Of course, some people might say, "Even if it's an illusion, it's still hard to let go" or "I *can't* let go—that's why I'm suffering."

I hear you. That feeling makes sense. And that's exactly why we need to practice the mindset the Buddha taught—to cleanse your mind. When you realize, "This is too painful. I want to live more freely," that's the moment you set out on your journey to a new way of living.

Suffering exists. But there is a way to remove it. In early Buddhism, this way was called *the path.*

> *A person who walks the path enters the darkness of life as if carrying a lamp into a pitch-black room. To find the path is to find the light of wisdom—the clarity of true understanding.*
>
> —***The Sutra of Forty-Two Chapters***

When you decide, "I'm going to let go of the judgments that create my suffering" and put that into practice, you are following the path. Isn't that a hopeful thought?

Instead of remaining trapped in the cycle of reacting, our life's goal should be to aim for freedom from it. Let go of the past. Let go of judgments. That's how you find peace.

There was a time in your life when you weren't suffering under the weight of judgment. It's time to return to that sense of freedom.

> *Wealth and beauty are not lasting treasures. What we desire often eludes us.*
>
> *But the path is always within our hearts. If we live by it, nothing can disturb our inner peace.*
>
> —**"Words of Encouragement to the Courtesan Ambapali,"**
> ***The Discourse on the Great Passing***

Beware the Trap of Ego

There is another kind of judgment that causes suffering—the kind where we tell ourselves, "I'm superior," "I'm right," "I'm better (or at least, I should be)." In Buddhism, this mindset is called *mana*, or simply "ego."

At first, ego feels good. It makes us feel confident, even powerful. But pride, arrogance and superiority all lead to disappointment, frustration and failure born from overconfidence. In the end, it's a losing game.

In truth, the best thing you can do is stop judging yourself and others altogether. Free up that mental energy for things that actually bring joy and fulfillment. When you do, you'll become a more open, relaxed version of yourself.

> *Thoughts of "I" and "they" are like arrows piercing the heart. Those who see clearly no longer cling to these illusions, and thus, they break free from suffering.*
>
> —**"Perception," *The Collection of Inspired Sayings***

The only question that matters

Ego is, at its core, an obsession with our own worth. It's not just arrogance—pride, vanity, even insecurity and low self-esteem all stem from the same attachment.

Deep down, we all believe our thoughts are correct. But

how do we even determine if our judgments are right or wrong?

The Buddha put it simply:

> *I only speak words that are beneficial.*
>
> *If something is true and beneficial, I will say it—even if the other person doesn't like hearing it—so long as the timing is right. This is because my words come from compassion.*
>
> —"The Buddha's Words to Prince Abhaya," *The Middle-Length Discourses*

Put another way, the Buddha's standards were simple: truthfulness and usefulness.

Sometimes, telling the truth isn't practical. But making choices based on whether your words will be useful is a standard we can apply anywhere.

Take work, for example. A useful decision can be one that boosts profits, creates a better work environment or improves efficiency. The key questions here are: "Does this help? Is it useful?"

Now, look at your everyday judgments—about yourself, others, your life, your job. About what's right and wrong, good or bad. Are they true? Are they useful?

Most of our judgments happen inside our heads. If they exist only in our thoughts, they are not true in any meaningful way. If they're not making life better, they're not useful, either.

So, what does that mean? That most of our judgments are neither true nor useful. They're just mental clutter.

As I mentioned earlier, judgment *feels good*. It also satisfies our desire for recognition. Together, those two things are the very essence of ego.

Step Away from the Mindset of Being Right

We all believe we're right—at least from our own perspective. But according to the Buddha's wisdom, the very act of believing "I'm right" is, in itself, mistaken.

In fact, the moment you judge yourself as being right, your judgment is already flawed. This is another fascinating truth the Buddha teaches us.

There is a well-known story from the early Buddhist scriptures that illustrates this point:

> *Once, in a distant city, a king gathered a group of people blind since birth and brought them to his palace. He had them touch different parts of an elephant—one felt the trunk, another the leg, another the tail. Then, the king asked, "Tell me, what is an elephant like?"*
>
> *One answered, "An elephant is like a long-handled plow." Another said, "No, it's like a stone pillar." Yet another insisted, "It's like a broom."*

> *Each person, having touched only one part of the elephant, was convinced they knew the truth. But when their descriptions didn't match, they started arguing—until the fight escalated into a brawl. The king, watching the chaos, burst into laughter.*
>
> —**"Sermon in the City of Savatthi,"** ***The Inspired Utterances***

Now, we must acknowledge that this story carries an outdated view of blindness. In ancient times, some people saw disabilities as a result of past-life karma, and this way of thinking still lingers in some traditional texts. That said, the story captures an essential truth—we only ever see a fraction of reality. We stand in different places, experience different things, and yet we act as if we have the whole picture. We convince ourselves we're right without realizing how limited our perspective really is.

Whenever we interact with others, differences in opinion are bound to arise. There are times when we feel, "No matter how you look at it, *I'm* the one who's right!" But that feeling—"no matter how you look at it"—comes entirely from our own way of thinking. And since we can only think with our own brain, of course, we'll always arrive at our own conclusion. That doesn't mean it's objectively correct. After all, everyone's background, experiences and even the way their minds work is different.

According to the Buddha, every judgment we make is just a passing thought in our own mind. It's nothing more than delusion, a trick of perception. Yet, when we cling to the idea that "I'm right," we immediately give birth to ego and the need to elevate oneself.

Buddhism teaches that true understanding isn't about proving you're right. Paradoxically, the deepest wisdom comes from not making rigid judgments at all. What really matters isn't being right but seeking what is true and beneficial.

This mindset is a beautiful thing. It dissolves stress, fosters mutual understanding, frees you from unnecessary reactions and allows you to contribute to the world in a more meaningful way.

> *Those who truly understand do not fall into the trap of believing, "I am right."*
>
> *As such, they do not get caught in the web of attachment that breeds suffering.*
>
> —**"Dialogue with a Brahmin,"** ***The Collection of Discourses***

Moving from Understanding to Action

Once you have grasped the wisdom of *not judging*, the next step is to put it into practice. Here we'll explore three life-changing ways to free yourself from unnecessary judgments:

1. Notice when your mind reacts with judgment.
2. Separate your thoughts from those of others.
3. Be open.

Each step supports the practice of not reacting, creating space for judgment-free awareness and clearer understanding.

The power of noticing "Oh, I just judged"

The first step is simple: *catch yourself in the act of judging.* Whenever a thought crosses your mind like, "Today isn't my day," "I totally messed up," "I really don't like that person" or "I'm such a failure," pause and acknowledge it. Say to yourself, "Oh, I just made a judgment."

We constantly evaluate people—deciding whether we like or dislike them, whether they're good or bad. The moment you notice yourself doing this, simply recognize it: "Ah, I'm judging again."

You might also find yourself engaged in casual discussions with friends or family, sharing opinions about others. When this happens, you can slip in a little self-awareness by saying something like, "Well, that's just my own opinion."

Some may wonder, "Is it wrong to judge someone as a good person?" Not necessarily—but keep in mind, positive judgments can easily flip to negative ones when circumstances change.

We also have to ask ourselves, who gave us the authority to decide who is good or bad in the first place? If the Buddha were here, he would probably shrug and say, "That's a judgment you don't need to make."

> *People lose themselves in constant judgment, failing to cultivate their own hearts.*
> *They let their eyes wander—but how does that serve them?*
> *Instead of chasing after what others think, turn inward and see yourself.*
>
> —"A Fellow Practitioner of Thera Kumarabhuta,"
> *The Verses of the Elder Monks*

The mindset shift: "I am who I am"

Next, *separate your thoughts from those of others.*

Judgment is a habit—one that's deeply ingrained in society. The world is full of people obsessed with comparisons, evaluations and gossip. In fact, gossip itself is nothing more than an endless parade of judgments.

But just because everyone else is doing it doesn't mean *you* have to. If you go along with the crowd, you'll end up just as tangled in judgment as they are. And, as we've seen, unnecessary judgment is the very thing that fuels suffering.

If you're serious about reducing your struggles, the answer

is clear: let go of judgment. Others may continue to judge, but if you truly want peace, you have to make a conscious choice—"I refuse to keep adding to my own suffering."

The Buddha once gave advice to a monk named Cunda on how to break free from misguided thinking. This was his response:

> *Cunda, remind yourself of this:*
>
> *Some may speak harshly, but I will make an effort to speak with kindness.*
>
> *Some may be trapped by their own opinions, but I will not be bound by mine.*
>
> *Some may cling to misconceptions, but I will strive for the right understanding.*
>
> *Some may be consumed by pride, but I will work to remain free from it.*
>
> *Some may obsess over their image, but I will live as my authentic self.*
>
> —**"The Discourse on Virtuous Conduct,"**
> ***The Middle-Length Discourses***

The Buddha's wisdom boils down to this: recognize that others may act a certain way, and that you don't have to follow suit. He draws a clear line—"Some people may do this, but I choose to do that."

That's one of the most empowering mindsets you can

adopt. Yes, there are people out there who thrive on judgment, but that doesn't mean you have to.

Your thoughts, your choices and your inner peace are entirely up to you. Think freely, decide independently and live on your own terms. That's the essence of the Buddha's way of thinking.

Be open

Another crucial key to freeing yourself from judgment is simple: *be open*. Not for anyone else's sake, but because it makes your own life easier.

When we cling to the belief that we're superior or always right, we start building walls between ourselves and others. It becomes harder to connect with people. Worse, whenever someone challenges us, we feel personally attacked—leading to anger, frustration or disappointment.

The problem, however, isn't other people. The real issue is our own stubborn belief that we're right.

For someone trapped by ego, letting go of the need to be right can feel like self-destruction—like giving up their very sense of identity. That's why it's so hard for those people to be open. This is where Buddhist wisdom comes in. Instead of obsessing over being right, we can shift our focus to *seeing the bigger picture*.

Seeing the bigger picture is part of what Buddhism calls

right thinking. It means stepping back and asking yourself, "Do I want to keep clinging to being right? Or do I want to let go and become someone more open, more understanding?"

Being *right* is nothing more than a tiny little ego boost. Who does it really make happy?

Wouldn't it be more fulfilling to be *open* rather than *right*? To genuinely listen to others, to be understanding, to have conversations where both hearts are willing to listen? Doesn't that sound like a happier way to live?

Being open invites happiness. People won't think less of you for it—in fact, they'll respect you more. And, most importantly, you'll feel more at ease.

The best thing you can do is to simply admit it to yourself: "I was caught up in my own pride." In Buddhist practice, there are moments dedicated to reflection and humility—times for recognizing our mistakes, our pride and our misunderstandings.

You don't have to make some grand, public confession—just make a quiet promise to yourself.

Try saying: "I'll work to be more open." Even that tiny shift in thinking can start to break down the barriers inside you and silence those once-automatic reactions.

Never Tear Yourself Down

At some point in life—whether at work, in relationships or just in general—you're going to feel like you've failed. The important thing is not to let it crush you. Never tear yourself down.

The problem is that our minds love to judge—especially ourselves. The moment we slip up, we think, "People must think less of me now," "Maybe I'm just not cut out for this" or "I'm such a failure."

For some, these thoughts spiral into deep insecurity, feelings of worthlessness or even the belief that life has no meaning. Sadly, in today's world, so many people suffer because they're trapped in their own continual self-judgment.

So, how do we break free? By building the kind of inner strength that won't let self-doubt take over.

You create your own anger

Let's take a closer look at the pain that comes from self-judgment.

When we judge ourselves harshly, we feel unworthy. And when we feel unworthy, anger starts to build. Since anger is an unpleasant emotion, we naturally want to get rid of it. That leads us to one of two instinctive reactions: attacking or escaping.

Attacking looks like lashing out, yelling, blaming others or turning the anger inward—beating yourself up, thinking you're worthless or even wanting to give up on life.

Escaping looks like avoiding reality by ignoring problems, procrastinating, cutting corners, shutting down emotionally, withdrawing from life, sleeping endlessly, falling into depression or numbing yourself with stimulating distractions or harmful habits.

Whenever we react in these ways, we, or the people around us, think, "This isn't good. I need to fix this."

Unfortunately, even that thought—"I need to fix this"—can turn into another layer of judgment. In other words, it can lead to the emergence of more anger, which, in turn, leads to new reactions of attacking or escaping. Once that happens, we're stuck in a vicious cycle.

Buddhist wisdom offers us a way out—by not creating anger in the first place.

No matter what happens, *choose not to judge*. Choose not to criticize. Choose not to reject yourself.

An Exercise for Reclaiming a Free Mind

So, how do we stop judging ourselves and others? How do we ensure we never fall into the trap of criticizing ourselves or those around us?

Most people don't know how to not judge. Sure, we understand the logic behind phrases like, "Don't be negative" or "Just accept things as they are," but when it comes down to it, our minds still whisper, "I need to do something about this."

Some people even take it a step further, worrying "What will the neighbors think?" or "What if people start talking behind my back?" These unnecessary fears and judgments create tension, and whether through words, facial expressions or even just a fleeting glance, other people pick up that negativity.

No matter whether the judgment comes from within or from those around you, there's only one thing to do: practice letting go of negative judgment. This isn't just a personal challenge—it's something everyone involved must commit to.

To tackle this, we can use the three steps I mentioned earlier that begin with noticing "Oh, I'm judging," but, in this exercise, let's focus specifically on those who struggle with self-judgment—those who instinctively put themselves (or others) down.

Here's how:

1. First, step outside and take a walk.
2. While there, take in the vast world around you.
3. Then, affirm yourself—think, "I accept myself."

These aren't just abstract ideas—they are the very practices I have relied on during the hardest moments of my own life. Let's break them down.

Step outside and walk

The first step is simple: get outside and walk. Whether for an hour, two hours or more, just keep walking for as long as you can.

As you do, shift your attention to what your body *feels*. Buddhism teaches that we experience the world through our five senses: sight, hearing, smell, taste and touch. Pay more attention to each of these as you walk than you do in your everyday life.

Notice how the sky looks different at dawn, in the afternoon and at night. The color of the trees, the reflections on the water, the glow of streetlights—what do you see in this exact moment? Open your eyes fully and observe the world around you.

Pay attention to the air as it enters your nostrils. Does it carry a scent? Does it feel cold, warm, humid, dry? The air outside is fresh and ever-changing—completely different from the stale thoughts trapped in your mind. Breathe it in. Let your sense of smell remind you that the world is alive.

Focus on the sensation of each step. Feel the ground through the soles of your shoes. Walk as far as you want—just keep moving forward.

Right now, your senses are all that truly exist. The worries and self-doubt that filled your mind earlier are nowhere to be found in this moment. Instead, there's just this—a new experience, a new version of you. You are already living a different life than before.

Try walking late at night or early in the morning, and you'll see convenience stores and 24-hour shops still open. Imagine the lives of the people working inside—each with their own struggles, their own stories. You'll realize something profound: everyone is alone in some way. And the moment you recognize another person's solitude, that's when you'll find that you yourself are not alone anymore.

If negative thoughts start creeping in, tell yourself, "These thoughts end here." Once self-criticism begins, it leads to a spiral of deluded thoughts. There are no answers in that darkness—only suffering.

So: *cut it off.* Redirect your awareness toward the world of sensation, to a different part of your mind—and step outside.

At Mount Hiei in Japan, monks undertake the legendary *Kaihogyo*—a grueling practice of walking between 30 and 80 kilometers a day for 7 years. It's a test of endurance, but also a path to enlightenment.

A simple walk to free yourself from self-judgment is also a form of practice. Don't think of it as a burden—think of it as an exercise, as a way of life, as something you do for yourself.

How long should you keep walking? There's no set answer. Fortunately, walking isn't complicated. Just keep going out and walking until the habit of self-judgment fades away completely.

There's nothing more important in life than freeing yourself from the thoughts that hold you back.

So, take a deep breath. Set your mind to it. And walk until you reclaim your freedom.

Take in the world around you

When you step outside and look around, you'll notice something—the world is full of people, all living their own lives. And here's a reality check: there aren't nearly as many people judging you as you might think. Look at a mother and child shopping together, a police officer on the street, a cashier at a store. These people are all absorbed in their own daily lives.

Most people aren't going around looking for someone to criticize—they're just trying to get through their own day. If you stop and ask for directions, you might be surprised by how caring and helpful people can be. The world is filled with kind, decent and compassionate people. Day or night, whenever you feel overwhelmed, look up at the sky. The world is vast. And yet, you may have been fixating on just one small thing—your self-judgment. Where did that judgment come from? Maybe from a parent, a passing comment from a friend or something you picked up from society's expectations. Maybe it was just a misunderstanding—a mistaken belief you've clung to for too long.

When we obsess over something, it naturally starts to seem huge, even all-consuming. It can feel like it defines our entire life. But step back. Recognize the obsession for what it is.

And then shift your focus outward—toward the bigger picture. When you do, you'll realize that the negative judgment that once felt so heavy is no longer there.

Lift your gaze to a new world. There, waiting for you, is a new life.

Affirm yourself

Another way to stop negating yourself is to simply use affirming words. Try saying, "I affirm myself."

Now, this idea of *affirmation* isn't the same as the *positive thinking* you so often hear about. People sometimes say things like, "I can do this!" or "I'm getting better every day!" as a form of self-motivation. But while such words can have a hypnotic effect, if they feel too far removed from reality, your mind will sense the disconnect. When that happens, affirmations lose their power, leaving you feeling left behind by your own words.

Buddhism is based on *right understanding*, so it doesn't rely on words that contradict reality or lean too much into wishful thinking (which can be seen as a kind of delusion). Of course, it's fine to have a vision for the future, but if it's nothing more than a fantasy, it remains just that—a fantasy.

The real issue is how to stop reacting to the self-negating judgments that creep into your mind in the moment. To do that, you need a simple phrase that halts the judgment itself.

That phrase is "I affirm myself." When you say it, you may feel your habitual judgments come to a stop.

From now on, whenever thoughts like "I'm useless," "I'll never be good enough" or "What's the point?" start creeping in, shut them down immediately by repeating this phrase. Say it over and over again: "I affirm myself."

When You Stop Judging, Life Starts Moving

Humans love to judge. We also crave validation. So, when reality isn't going the way we want, it's easy—almost instinctive, even—to slip into self-negation.

But from a Buddhist perspective, self-negation has no logical basis—it only creates suffering, and it's nothing more than a delusion. The Buddha's view is that judgments that aren't true or beneficial are simply unnecessary.

You might argue, "But isn't it sometimes necessary to push yourself harder? Doesn't self-criticism help you improve?" Buddhism offers a different approach. Instead of using self-criticism or anger as fuel, it emphasizes finding your direction, focusing on the present and taking action rather than dwelling on negative thoughts. This approach allows you to keep moving forward without the burden of self-negation.

No matter your situation, let go of the urge to judge yourself. Instead, focus on what you can do in the moment and act accordingly.

During my time at a Zen monastery, a young monk once overslept and arrived late to the morning service. Devastated, he muttered, "I'm not cut out to be a monk . . ."

But the head monk wasn't having any of it. He shouted, "Fool! Focus only on the now!"

Here, the head monk was demonstrating *right thinking.* Clinging to the past and using it as a reason to negate the present is a mental trap—a distraction from what truly matters, and a source of inner turmoil.

Life is full of missteps and failures. What matters is how you respond to them.

Don't dwell on your mistakes. Don't beat yourself up. Don't look back in regret. Don't give in to pessimism. Instead, focus on the present, understand it correctly and dedicate yourself to what you can do right now.

Of course, if you've hurt someone, it's important to acknowledge it and sincerely apologize. Doing this is part of taking responsibility. Embrace that moment and take the opportunity to start afresh.

Let go of the stains of the past and refrain from creating new ones. When you awaken to true wisdom, you break free from assumptions and stop blaming yourself.

Seek to understand both your inner world and the world around you, but never measure your worth by what you perceive. That kind of thinking does not lead to joy.

Don't judge yourself as superior, inferior or equal to others. No matter what people say, don't let their words define your value.

True joy comes when all cravings, judgments and comparisons disappear. At that point, you will have already won—no one can defeat you anymore.

—**"On Disputes" and "Swift Accomplishment,"**
The Collection of Discourses

How to Cultivate True Confidence

Many people think, "If only I had more confidence, my life would be better." But from a Buddhist standpoint, confidence itself is just another judgment.

Since judgment is a type of delusion, it can vanish in an instant. The moment you face a tough reality, your confidence can crumble. You might find yourself doubting yourself, hesitating or feeling overwhelmed.

Instead of chasing confidence, Buddhism suggests something far more practical—do what needs to be done. Focus on action, not self-evaluation.

By shifting your focus from "Am I confident or not?" to "What can I do right now?" you'll naturally produce better results than someone who simply relies on confidence.

That is the Buddha's approach to strength and self-mastery.

Seeking confidence is irrational

Saying "I wish I had more confidence" is, from a Buddhist perspective, a completely irrational thought. Why? Because confidence is essentially a judgment—"I can do this" or "I'll definitely succeed." But at any given moment, you don't actually know if you can do something or if you'll succeed. There's no way to make that judgment in advance.

Even if you've succeeded once before, circumstances always change. There's no guarantee you'll succeed next time. So even if you say, "That success gave me confidence," that confidence is meaningless in a new situation.

In short, having confidence in advance is simply not possible.

Look at the business world or professional sports—high achievers rarely, if ever, say, "I have confidence." If someone does, most people think, "They're in for a rude awakening."

You don't need to think about confidence. The future is uncertain. Instead, focus on what needs to be done in the moment—that's the right mindset. This isn't just a Buddhist concept—it's a truth many people understand on an instinctive level.

So, What Can I Do Right Now?

Why do so many people still crave confidence? Because they're caught up in delusion.

The first delusion is the desire to believe "I can do this"—a form of ego. You've probably met people who have an inflated sense of pride or look down on others without any real reason.

They might seem confident, but, in reality, they're just clinging to the delusion of thinking of themselves as amazing, or else desperately wanting others to see them that way. This kind of confidence lacks a firm basis in reality.

The second delusion comes from wanting to erase anxiety and fear. People worry, "What if I can't do it?" "What if I fail?" "What if things go wrong?" These fears about the future, which are also delusions, make them think, "If only I had confidence." Any confidence born from this mindset, however, is just another delusion meant to cover up anxiety. In the end, both so-called confident people and those who lack confidence are stuck in self-serving delusions.

Someone who has internalized a Buddhist way of thinking would immediately recognize that delusions aren't reliable. When feelings of confidence arise, they would think, "Oh, that's just another delusion" and reset their mindset. Instead, they would ask themselves, "What can I do right now?"—which is the rational way of thinking that the Buddha taught.

However, most people who crave confidence don't realize they're chasing after a delusion. Instead, they try to pile new delusions on top of old ones.

Those who start with the delusion "I'm great, I can do this" create an even bigger delusion of "I can do even more." On the other hand, those who start with "I can't do this" hold on to that delusion while trying to counter it with a new one—"If only I were more capable, I could do it."

Either way, both these types of people are just building new delusions from old ones. It's an error in thinking, nothing more.

Let go of the "I have to try harder" mindset

Buddhism doesn't bother with those who say "I can do it" without reason. Such people will eventually hit a wall and realize they were mistaken, and maybe that's when they will become open to learning.

What's more important is understanding the mindset of those who say, "I lack confidence, so I need more of it."

The truth is that the initial belief—"I don't have confidence"—is already a mistake. Even if you've faced repeated failures, that doesn't mean you need to feel a lack of confidence. There's something else you should be focusing on instead, which I'll explain shortly.

"I lack confidence" and "I'm not good enough yet" are

unnecessary judgments—they are those misapprehensions we met earlier. If you don't realize that, you may hesitate on important decisions, push yourself too hard trying to *gain* confidence or keep chasing new qualifications or achievements to prove yourself.

Delaying action won't suddenly make you feel confident, and pushing yourself harder or achieving more won't necessarily do it, either.

Why? Because your entire thought process started with a negative delusion—"I'm not good enough." If you don't break free from that, you'll always be chasing after confidence without ever truly feeling it.

Many people feel like they're not quite "there" yet—like they still have further to go. But that very thought is an unnecessary judgment—yet another delusion. Instead of reacting to those feelings, the important thing is to focus on what you *need* to do right now, and what you *can* do right now.

Stop thinking, "I'm not good enough." Stop thinking, "I want more confidence." Affirm yourself as you are. Then, do what you can, in the here and now.

All You Need to Do Is Gain Experience

In any field, people say it takes about ten years to gain a real sense of expertise. Whether it's business, sports or the arts, success usually comes after many years of learning skills, building experience and dedicated practice. Top performers often spend a decade or more honing their craft before they truly shine. No matter where you look, investing time and effort is essential for achieving mastery. At this moment in time, you don't need to judge anything. Just take action. Gain experience.

Let's break it down into steps:

1. Give something a try.
2. Accumulate experience.
3. Start achieving small results.
4. Earn recognition from others.
5. See for yourself what works and what doesn't.

Some people may find the first step—give something a try—difficult. If that's you, ask yourself, "Is this just another delusion?" Are you hesitating because of thoughts like "I might fail," "I might inconvenience others" or "I'm not ready yet"? If so, those are merely delusions.

Don't react to them. Instead, recognize them for what they are, and then simply decide to start.

If you can adopt this mindset, your work life and your personal life will become that much easier.

If you don't know what to do, ask, "What should I do next?"

If you don't know how to do something, ask, "How do I do this?"

If someone helps you, say, "Thank you."

If you make a mistake, say, "I'm sorry."

And then, get started with the mindset of "I'll give it my best shot."

Such a mindset—where you don't obsess over whether you'll succeed or fail—could be seen as a Buddhist approach to life. But, in my view, this way of thinking is incredibly useful no matter what job you have or what field you're in.

You start something, little by little you get better at it, you gain experience and, one day, when you look back, you realize, "Wow, I've come this far." You reach a point where you can see real progress, where results aren't just possible—they're inevitable.

This mindset—of taking consistent steps without being thrown off by setbacks or self-criticism—is at the heart of the practice we've explored in this chapter. By letting go of unnecessary judgments, you create the space for real growth, confidence and lasting change, and can step into the next stage of freeing yourself from the pain of negative emotions.

CHAPTER 3

DON'T LOSE OUT TO NEGATIVE EMOTIONS

Keeping Your Emotions Steady

NOW THAT YOU'VE stopped judging and putting yourself and others down, let's explore how emotions are simply another form of the mind's reactions—and why developing wisdom around them is the crucial next step in the path to freedom from unnecessary suffering. By learning to steady your emotions, you build the foundation for deeper calm, clearer thinking and greater resilience. After all, emotional struggles are part of everyday life. Learning to manage them is therefore essential to mastering the practice of not reacting.

At work, at home, wherever you go, emotions can catch you off guard. Stress piles up. Anger makes it impossible to focus. A mistake at work leaves you feeling defeated. Losing something precious fills you with sadness. Uncertainty about the future stirs anxiety. This constant inner turmoil is your emotions at work.

Who wouldn't want to master their emotions, to handle them smoothly instead of being ruled by them?

Ultimately, emotions are just another reaction of the mind—let's explore the wisdom that helps us stop letting them get the better of us.

Organizing Your Worries

According to Buddhism, we can break down emotional distress into two main categories:

1. Preventing unpleasant emotions from arising in the first place, and if they do arise, learning how to reset or resolve them quickly.
2. Figuring out how to interact with others.

This distinction lies at the very heart of the practice of not reacting. Recognizing that managing your inner emotional world and navigating your relationships require different approaches is crucial for true transformation.

In fact, most people inadvertently mix up these two forms of distress. When we get angry, our minds immediately focus on the person who triggered that anger—what they said, what they did. From there, it's just a battle of emotions and thoughts of "I'm right" and "They're wrong," leading to an endless cycle of conflict and suffering.

People often say, "Relationships are the source of all my problems." But from a Buddhist perspective, that isn't entirely accurate. Wrestling with our emotions and struggling with how to interact with others are two separate challenges.

By understanding and practicing how to pause before reacting emotionally, we gain the power to break free from these cycles.

Let's start by addressing our emotions. What wisdom does the Buddha offer on this score?

The Greatest Victory Is Not Reacting

The key to avoiding unnecessary emotions is simple: don't react in the first place. The Buddha, a master of non-reaction, demonstrates this principle in the following story:

> *Over time, the Buddha gained great renown in ancient India, his teachings earning him the name the "Awakened One." Even prominent Brahmins, who had hundreds of disciples of their own, found many of their followers wishing to study instead under the Buddha. In India, both then as now, the caste system holds absolute significance. The Buddha belonged to the warrior class, which ranks below the Brahmins, the priestly class. For a Brahmin of the highest*

> *caste to become a disciple of the Buddha—that was a shock of the highest order at the time.*
>
> *One day, a proud Brahmin learned that someone from his own caste had joined the Buddha's disciples—a fact he found utterly unacceptable. Enraged, he stormed into the Buddha's presence, right in front of a crowd of disciples and visitors, unleashing a torrent of insults and slander. The atmosphere grew incredibly tense.*
>
> *But the Buddha remained calm, responding with a simple question—"Brahmin, if you prepare a meal for a guest, but the guest refuses to eat it, who does the meal belong to?"*
>
> *The Brahmin had no choice but to answer. "Well, it remains mine."*
>
> *"And what do you do with that meal?" the Buddha asked.*
>
> *"I suppose I would eat it myself," the Brahmin replied.*
>
> *Then the Buddha said, "If someone hurls insults at another, and the other does not accept them, those insults remain with the one who gave them. I do not accept your words. Take them back with you."*
>
> —"Confrontation with an Abusive Brahmin,"
> *The Connected Discourses*

In this story, the *meal* represents the Brahmin's insults. By refusing to engage, the Buddha avoided being consumed by anger. He simply didn't *eat* what was being served.

The Buddha responded with *no reaction* even when faced with something that would normally anger most other people.

This was because he knew that if your life goal is to achieve a mind free of suffering, then reacting and allowing your heart to be disturbed by unpleasant emotions would be utterly pointless. No matter the situation, he never reacted—he simply focused on the other person and sought to understand them.

From this, we learn a profound lesson: *victory isn't about defeating others, but rather about not losing yourself to emotional reactions.*

Let others handle their own reactions

This story also teaches us another key insight: we should let others be responsible for their own reactions.

The Brahmin in the story, believing himself to have been born to a higher caste, was driven by arrogance, jealousy and a desire to defeat the Buddha. A typical response would have been to argue, fight back or try to prove him wrong. But arguments are nothing more than two egos clashing—both sides believing they are right and trying to assert their own positions. The psychology behind arguing is all about pushing your own narrative to satisfy your desire for recognition.

The Buddha, however, took a different approach. He understood that what is *right* is subjective, which was why he didn't try to convince the Brahmin of anything. Instead, he simply acknowledged the Brahmin's perspective without getting entangled in it.

Of course, there are times when we need to resolve conflicts. But that, ultimately, is a problem of relationships and engaging with others, which we'll address later. For now, let's focus on mastering the art of not reacting to negative emotions.

People are wired differently, so it's only natural that we think differently. And yet, deep down, we tend to assume that others should think like us, or at least that they're capable of it. But this expectation—this belief—is another delusion.

On top of that, the need to be right, the urge to make others see things our way, is often fueled by that same ego we discussed in the previous chapter. That's why, when someone challenges our opinion, it can feel like they're rejecting us as a person. And what do we do? We react with anger. This is also why people who lack self-assurance tend to get angry more easily.

This kind of mental state is a trap—a mix of delusion and ego that keeps us stuck in irrational thinking. The key is to hit the reset button and shift to a mindset based on right understanding. That looks like accepting the simple truth that your reactions and other people's reactions are entirely separate things.

Learning to separate the two is a game changer. Let others own their reactions, and don't take them on as your burden. This is the basis for avoiding trouble in interpersonal relationships.

How to Cut Your Worries in Half

If you let go of the need to control how others react, you instantly slash your worries in half. From there, if you can also work on not reacting yourself, emotional stress will start to lose its grip on you.

Of course, that's easier said than done. A lot of people struggle with knee-jerk reactions—flaring up in anger or snapping back with a retort. So, what's the trick to keeping your cool?

Here's a method worth trying. Use half your mind to focus forward, and the other half to stay anchored inward.

First, picture your mind split into two parts: a front half and a back half. Close your eyes and imagine:

1. The front half of your mind is outward-facing, focused on what's in front of you.
2. The back half is turned inward, quietly observing your own inner state.

Now, let the front half do its job—it takes in what the other person is saying, but it doesn't react. It just listens. Your only task is to understand. If you get what they're saying, you acknowledge it and say, "I see." If you don't, you either ask for clarification or simply recognize, "I don't understand this right now."

Sometimes, you might find yourself thinking, "I have no idea what this person is talking about!" But if they're speaking a language you know, you should be able to grasp the words. So, what's really happening? Chances are that a part of you is *refusing* to understand. Your mind might be tangled up in thoughts like, "I'm right," "They should do it this way" or "I've heard *this* before." These thoughts stir up frustration, making it hard to clearly see the other person or their point of view.

And let's be honest, there are people you just don't *want* to understand. Perhaps it's your parents, a difficult boss or that one person who always gets under your skin. But those are exactly the situations in which practicing non-reaction can be the most powerful. Instead of getting pulled in, try this approach: acknowledge their words neutrally—"I hear you"—and then ask yourself, "What is it they actually want?" Keep your stance objective, not emotional.

Meanwhile, the back half of your brain is doing something equally important—it's watching your own reactions. Are you getting irritated? Are old memories creeping in? Is doubt or tension bubbling up? These kinds of reactions are completely normal. Just noticing these things without getting swept away by them can make all the difference.

In Zen philosophy, there is a concept called *fudoshin*—the *immovable mind*. It's not about having no emotions—it's about being so aware of them that they no longer control you, and it's only achievable by keeping a close eye on your own mind.

After all, the mind never truly stops moving. It keeps running until the day you die—or until you reach enlightenment, or *nibbana*. This is perfectly natural. The key is to train yourself to watch this ever-moving mind, to be aware of it and to stop any further reactions beyond that. This is the essence of cultivating an immovable mind.

Even the slightest lapse in the back half of your awareness can lead to you getting sucked into a storm of unhelpful emotions—anger, fear, doubt, resentment, frustration. It can bring on delusion and, consequently, sadness. Suddenly, you're drowning in thoughts like, "How dare they?," "This is so unfair!" or "I can't believe this is happening again!"

That's why the goal isn't to avoid discomfort but to keep it from taking over. The more you practice not reacting, the more you develop an immovable mind—an unshakable mind that doesn't get hijacked by every passing emotion.

Why Did the Yakuza Cry?

One morning, while I was helping with a food drive for the homeless in a Tokyo park, a commotion broke out. A few volunteers ran up, their expressions tense. "There's a man causing trouble!" they said. I hurried toward the source of the disturbance.

Over 200 homeless individuals had gathered, watching from a distance as a man, clearly drunk, caused a scene. He wore an all-black tracksuit with bold red calligraphy down the right sleeve reading, "Benevolence, Justice, Courtesy, Wisdom, Faith." His tanned, shaved head bore the unmistakable marks of a yakuza—a member of one of Japan's organized crime syndicates.

The man stormed toward the large pot of curry we had prepared, yelling, "I'll flip this whole damn thing over!"

I stepped in front of him. His bloodshot eyes widened as he barked at me, "Hey, monk! You picking a fight with me?!"

I gave him a slight smile. "Let's talk first."

"This whole food drive of yours—it's just a bunch of hypocritical crap!"

"Maybe so."

"What can *you* possibly do for these people?"

"Maybe nothing."

I didn't argue. I didn't contradict him. I just listened.

Before long, five police officers arrived. One of the volunteers had called them.

"Who the hell called the cops?!" the man roared, now turning his anger toward them.

A heated back-and-forth ensued, but even he knew he couldn't win against the police. They grabbed his arm, preparing to take him in.

I stood between him and the officers, listening as the tension in his voice cracked and, for a brief moment, his tough exterior slipped away. "My mum . . . she's in prison," he confessed quietly.

Then, his eyes filled with tears.

"I see. Have you gone to visit her?" I asked.

"No," he said, his voice trembling.

"Have you written her a letter?"

"I . . . I can't write properly," he sobbed, his voice breaking with emotion.

"I see. Then let's write one together. We'll do it when you get back from the station."

"You'd help me?" he asked meekly. "But . . . I don't even know what to say."

"Just start with, *Thanks for bringing me into this world.* That's enough. We'll figure the rest out together. I'll be waiting."

The man didn't resist as the officers led him away.

That night, he returned. We sat and talked for hours. He had never finished secondary school. He truly couldn't write. His mother and father had both lived hard lives, and he hadn't seen his mother in nearly 20 years. He survived doing grunt work for the yakuza, drinking to drown out his loneliness.

That night, we became friends.

If I had responded with anger or hostility that morning, the situation would have exploded. And I never would have seen the man's tears or his honest feelings.

He still calls me sometimes. And I believe the only reason

we stayed connected is because, in that moment, I followed the Buddha's teachings:

Don't react. First, seek to understand.

We all encounter difficult, even combative people. But if we respond with the same energy they bring—anger for anger, hostility for hostility—it turns into an endless cycle.

The real danger isn't losing the argument. It's losing yourself in the reaction.

When you find yourself on the verge of snapping back, take a deep breath. Exhale. Make a conscious decision—"I'll try to understand first."

At the same time, use the other part of your awareness to watch your own reactions. Observe: "Am I getting irritated?," "Am I dredging up past grudges?," "Is fear or doubt creeping in?" Just noticing these things helps you stay grounded.

This approach isn't easy. But if you want to stay true to yourself—and maybe even connect with the person across from you—it's worth the effort.

Half your awareness should be on understanding the other person. The other half should be on staying aware of your own reactions. Let that be your guiding principle.

How to Deal with Difficult People

After learning to avoid emotional reactions, the next step on our path is figuring out how to engage with difficult people.

From a Buddhist perspective, *engagement* means deciding what kind of mindset you bring into an interaction. One of the hallmarks of the Buddha's teachings is the emphasis on self-awareness—always questioning your own thoughts and approach rather than focusing on controlling or changing others.

By consciously choosing the mindset you direct toward someone, you can create a way of living that isn't burdened by toxic relationships or unnecessary suffering.

Let's dive into the fundamental principles for dealing with difficult people so you can do just that:

1. Avoid judging others.
2. Let go of the past.
3. Always see the person as "new."
4. Focus on mutual understanding.
5. Keep an eye on the ultimate goal of your interactions.

Avoid judging others

Avoiding judgment is simply putting into practice what you learned in Chapter 2 about not jumping to conclusions.

When negative emotions arise, it's tempting to slap a label on someone: "What a jerk," "How inconsiderate," "I can't believe them," "They never change," "I'm done with this person." Our minds rush to these conclusions because they offer a sense of control.

Sometimes, these judgments may even feel justified. After all, there are people out there whose behavior would be considered thoughtless by any metric.

But that doesn't mean our judgments aren't built on shaky ground.

This is because harsh judgments are often driven by our own ego—a desire for approval or to feel *right*. Complaining about someone or mentally writing them off often serves as a way to boost our own self-worth, but, in the long run, this only fuels unnecessary negativity.

From a Buddhist standpoint, the goal is to keep your mind clear and unburdened. That being the case, why waste mental energy on judging someone when it only adds to your own stress?

The most important thing for us as human beings is not to store up suffering in the heart. No matter how much happiness we achieve, suffering (in the form of reactions) can always come along and ruin it.

So, if a judgment leads to more suffering, it's better to let it go. When you keep replaying thoughts like, "They're such a mess" or "They're going to have a miserable life with that attitude," the only one you're harming is yourself.

And let's not forget, it's also unfair to the other person. The more judgments we make, the less room we leave for the possibility of understanding. Even if it seems unlikely right now, there is always a chance for connection. But if we keep making snap judgments, if we condemn the other person before we give ourselves a chance to know them, we'll shut that door before it even has a chance to open.

The bottom line is that judgment brings a whole lot of unnecessary baggage. And the closer the relationship—the more important the other person is to you—the more damage your judgments can do.

I don't claim to be right.

I recognize that attachment to opinions is just that—attachment.

I understand the mistakes others make, but I do not allow myself to be consumed by them.

Instead, I observe my own mind and maintain clarity and peace.

—**"Response to a Brahmin,"** ***The Collection of Discourses***

Let go of the past

The next key principle in dealing with difficult people is not to drag the past into the present. People have a habit of clinging to old memories and filtering their current interactions through them. The problem is, those old memories often trigger fresh anger, making the situation even worse.

> *He who thinks, "They insulted me," "They defeated me," "They took from me," will never cease to resent, because his anger is born from his own memories.*
>
> —"A Pair of Verses," *The Path of the Dhamma*

From a Buddhist perspective, *clinging to the past* means *reacting to memory*. This is a crucial concept to grasp.

Let's say you had an argument with someone. At first, your anger was directed at them. But after they leave, you're still fuming. If you're stuck replaying the argument in your head—feeling more frustrated by the minute—what is actually causing your suffering?

Not the other person.

It's *your own memory* that's keeping you upset.

When you get caught up in thoughts like, "I can't believe they said that!" or "They're always like this!," you're reacting not to the person, but to the memory of them. That's why your anger doesn't go away—it's being fueled by your own mind.

If you master the art of non-reaction, you will avoid getting stuck in old memories and find that anger dissolves effortlessly. This might sound like a big ask, but it's not—it could be as simple as stepping into the bathroom for a few minutes, looking at the wall behind the other person or even just shifting your focus. These techniques, at the very least, will allow you to walk away from a conflict without carrying it with you.

The next time an unpleasant memory resurfaces, pay attention to your reaction to it. If you're still upset even after the situation is over, remind yourself, "This is just a memory. The one reacting is me—the other person isn't even here." Stay calm and focus on soothing your emotions.

Always see the other party as "new"

"Memories are just memories. Don't let them trigger you." This might just be one of the greatest insights Buddhism has to offer.

There is another key principle when dealing with conflict or challenging behaviors in others: see them as a new person every time you interact with them.

In Buddhism, everything, including people and their minds, is considered *impermanent*—nothing stays the same.

Here's a simple experiment. Close your eyes and try to focus on just one thought—maybe a work project or a future goal. Set a timer for five minutes and keep your mind on that one thing.

Now, when the timer goes off, check in—what are you thinking about? Chances are that your mind has wandered off to something completely different.

If the widely reported claim that the human brain generates about 70,000 thoughts per day is true, that equates to roughly one new thought every 1.2 seconds. Our minds are constantly shifting, restless and fluid. This is a clear example of impermanence in action.

If the human mind is impermanent, then so, too, are people.

Most of us assume that people stay the same. You expect the friend you saw yesterday to be the same person today. But the truth is, while their body, name, job or home may be the same, their mind isn't. And if their mind has changed, can we really say they're the same person?

We hold on to past memories and judgments—"That's just how they are" or "I'm this kind of person"—and interact with people based on those fixed ideas. But, in reality, every interaction is new because every time we meet a person *they* are new.

Assuming that people remain the same is a misconception, a kind of unspoken rule meant to keep the relationship going. Even *you* aren't the same person you were yesterday. Your thoughts, feelings and perspectives have shifted, even in subtle ways. So why wouldn't the same be true for everyone else?

If we truly grasp this, then the person in front of us is *always* a fresh version of themselves. Thinking of someone as "that person who wronged me" is just our own attachment. We have the power to choose to meet them as if for the first time.

Try making it a rule in your relationships: "Next time we meet, let's start fresh."

Focus on mutual understanding

Another essential principle when it comes to dealing with difficult people is *mutual understanding.* After all, not reacting doesn't mean ignoring the person or just gritting your teeth through difficult interactions.

Some people suffer in silence, tolerating mistreatment because they don't want to upset anyone, disrupt the workplace or hurt the relationship. While this may seem considerate, what this really means is they're suppressing their own anger. And that anger doesn't just disappear—it builds up. Over time, it becomes unbearable, even leading to burnout or depression.

This is why it's important to shift the focus. Instead of just suppressing emotions, again try splitting your attention: one half of your mind should be focused on understanding the other person, and the other half should be watching your own reactions. This way, you avoid getting swept up in emotion while still making an effort to connect.

Another key shift is recognizing that mutual understanding is the foundation of any meaningful relationship. There is nothing more important than getting the other person to understand your own feelings, ideas and thoughts. Expressing yourself—telling the other person, "This is how I feel" or "This is what I think"—is one of the most constructive things you can do.

If the other person refuses to listen or make an effort to

understand, you might need to rethink the relationship. After all, no healthy relationship should be built on one-sided pain. But if there is even a *chance* that the other person can understand, then that's where you should direct your energy.

The key is to communicate clearly, to explain. If something bothers you, say so. If you need them to stop a certain behavior, tell them. That's your part of the equation. How they respond is up to them. Give them time, observe and see what happens. What's important is that both parties recognize the need to understand and be understood by the other.

Understanding takes time. There's no need to rush it. Approach the situation with optimism and trust—not necessarily in the other person, but in your own ability to navigate the relationship wisely. After all, trusting is a choice *we* make. When mutual understanding is achieved, emotions reset and the relationship transforms.

Keep an eye on the ultimate goal of your interactions

In Buddhism, a lot of emphasis is placed on direction. Where are you headed in life? Where is this relationship going?

Seeking mutual understanding is a direction. Wanting to be heard and understood is a direction. One direction you *don't* want to take is a relationship built on endless conflict and resentment. That's not a goal—it's a trap.

Sometimes, people get stuck in a cycle of mutual suffering, repeating the same conflicts over and over, never questioning why they're engaging in this struggle. They become attached to their own perspective, their expectations, their conveniences, their demands, convinced that they're right and the other person is wrong.

This is where Buddhist wisdom comes in. The Buddha taught that attachment itself is the source of suffering. It's not enough to understand this concept intellectually—you have to wake up to the reality that constant conflict isn't serving you, that you are causing each other pain.

Instead, keep in mind the ultimate goal of your interactions. Tell yourself this: "Neither of us is in this relationship to suffer. We're here to understand, to grow and to support each other's happiness."

The Golden Rule: Prioritize Joy

There's one last thing I want you to keep in mind when it comes to not reacting and keeping your emotions steady: prioritizing joy.

When you learn not to react impulsively to every situation, you create an opportunity to notice and nurture positive emotions rather than being caught in cycles of frustration or anger.

Everyone wants to be happy, but what *is* happiness, exactly? According to Buddhism, happiness is directly tied to our internal state:

- Pleasant emotions—ease, joy or excitement—reflect a state of mind of happiness (*sukha*).
- Unpleasant emotions—anger, fear or frustration—reflect a state of mind of unhappiness (*dukkha*).

This isn't a uniquely Buddhist idea—it's wired into all living beings. Some primitive organisms literally change color depending on whether they're experiencing comfort (pleasure) or danger (pain). More complex creatures, including humans, produce different hormones based on their emotional state.

In short, *every living thing* is navigating a world of joy and pain. Humans are no different. Babies laugh when they're comfortable and cry when they aren't. From birth, our lives are guided by these two fundamental responses: toward joy and away from pain.

Buddhism often uses the terms *joy* and *pain* in conjunction with *happiness* and *unhappiness* (*sukha* and *dukkha*). (There is also a third state—*neutral [adukkhamasukha]*—meaning neither pleasant nor unpleasant. For most people, however, neutral quickly turns into boredom, which is just another form of discomfort.)

Ultimately, the human mind oscillates between these two states of joy and pain. As such, the guiding principle for a fulfilling life is simple:

- If you want happiness, prioritize the experiences and responses that bring you joy.
- If you want to avoid suffering, train yourself not to react in ways that bring you pain.

Wait, it's okay to chase after your desires?

What does it mean to prioritize pleasant reactions?

Living beings feel joy when their desires are fulfilled. That means the fastest path to happiness is to acknowledge your desires, accept them without resistance and fulfill them.

For example, eating what you love and truly enjoying it, getting a good night's sleep, spending time with family, valuing sensory pleasures like hobbies, entertainment, the feeling of something delicious, fun or soothing—these are all ways in which we find sensory pleasure.

When I say this, some people respond with, "But I thought Buddhism was all about self-denial and strict discipline?" It's true that if your goal is to achieve the ultimate peace—*nibbana*, where all reactions of the mind cease—then you would need to eliminate all reactions, both pleasant and unpleasant. There is indeed a strict path within Buddhism that leads to such a realm. But *nibbana* is just one approach. It's not a universal goal that applies to everyone.

Buddhist wisdom offers practical tools that anyone can

use, regardless of their beliefs or background. You don't have to fully commit to Buddhism as a religion or philosophy to benefit from its insights. What we all share as individuals is the desire to escape suffering and achieve our own personal happiness. As long as we think in that direction, that's enough.

And, in fact, the Buddha's teachings were built around just such an open-ended purpose—helping people find happiness in a way that suits them.

Desire is a tool that can be put to use

In the practice of not reacting, it's essential to develop an awareness of your own desires and how they influence your mind.

If pleasure is worth valuing, then desires that bring you pleasure should also be valued. That includes the desire to be recognized and appreciated by others. For example, if your drive to succeed at work, be praised or be appreciated fuels your motivation, then there's no reason to reject that desire. It serves a purpose.

So, if you have an urge to try something new, to take on a challenge, honor that feeling. Even if your motivation is something like, "I want to make money," "I want to be on top" or "I want to win," as long as the pursuit itself brings you joy, go for it.

But here's the catch. Remember the cycle we looked at in

Chapter 1—where a craving becomes an unquenchable thirst that fuels an endless cycle of suffering? Desires only lead to happiness if they genuinely bring you pleasure. If your desire spirals out of control—turning into anxiety, frustration or restlessness because you're not getting results, not getting recognition—then it's time to let that desire go. The Buddha's insights tell us, "If it causes suffering, take a step back and reassess."

People's lives tend to fall into two categories: those spent chasing desires in a way that causes suffering, and those spent cherishing the desires that bring joy.

Living in a way that breaks the cycle, transforms desire into energy and fosters joy is rational.

Staying stuck in the cycle, chasing unnecessary desires and being overwhelmed by discomfort is irrational.

We all want to live happily. That's why it's essential to regularly check in with yourself and ask, "Am I feeling joy right now or am I feeling pain?" If you find yourself in discomfort, follow the Buddha's example—reset your reactions.

Increase joy, reduce unhappiness

When you make it a habit to fully embrace your daily moments of joy—sincerely acknowledging "This is fun!" or "This feels great!"—your ability to recognize joy will sharpen and become more astute.

Happiness isn't something fixed—it can be cultivated

through practice. As a monk, I make a daily effort to refine my awareness—through Zen, mindfulness and conscious observation. I focus on the sensations throughout my body—the feeling of my feet against the ground, the rise and fall of my breath. This practice keeps my mind fresh, engaged and never bored.

By becoming more aware of your emotional responses and learning how to gently guide them using the techniques in this chapter, you will reduce discomfort and build a more peaceful, fulfilling life—exactly the kind of freedom from mental turmoil that this book aims to help you achieve.

Now that you've freed yourself from the pain of negative emotions, it's time to release the pressure of other people's opinions.

CHAPTER 4

BREAKING FREE FROM THE EYES OF OTHERS

Stop Chasing Others' Approval

We all wonder from time to time, "What do they think of me?" However, constantly worrying about other people's opinions keeps your mind trapped in reactive patterns. It keeps you on edge, always nervous and self-conscious. The fear of judgment creates tension and pressure, leading to mistakes at crucial moments. A casual remark can cut deep, and even a fleeting glance can spiral into paranoia—"Are they laughing at me?"

Wouldn't it be freeing to stop caring so much about how others see you?

If the Buddha, the ultimate master of inner freedom, were here, he would have the following to say: "Why do we get so caught up in what others think?"

Why Do We Care About Others' Opinions?

If we flip this question and imagine a situation where we feel completely at ease in front of others, the answer becomes clear. For instance, if you believe "this person likes me" or "they think highly of me," you feel naturally relaxed. In other words, the real culprit behind this anxiety is, once again, the desire for approval.

Take this example. Let's say someone grows up as the third of five siblings—stuck in the middle, neither the eldest nor the youngest. They never received much attention from their parents. As a result, they crave recognition. They become obsessed with fashion, build a vast social network and establish themselves as a social butterfly. Yet, they're constantly plagued by the nagging question, "How do people see me?" At its core, this anxiety stems from a deep desire for approval.

Wanting approval is natural. The problem lies in why we seek validation and how this desire leads to obsession over others' opinions. The process looks like this. You want to be recognized—you're fixated on proving your worth—and this sparks a chain of thoughts: "Are they judging me? Do they think I'm good enough? What if they don't like me?" This constant speculation about how others see you is a delusion. It's a mental story your mind creates, an imagined reality that keeps you trapped in fear and anxiety. The fear of judgment isn't rooted in actual facts, but in this self-generated, distorted narrative born from the desire for approval.

Worries like "How am I perceived at work?," "Did I upset them?," "Have I lost their trust?"—these are all projections fueled by our attachment to self-worth.

When this illusion runs wild, it turns into paranoia. You start believing you're disliked, mocked or talked about behind your back. Some people even begin to see everyone around them as an enemy. It's a painful way to live. And because it feels real to the person experiencing it, it's a difficult trap to escape.

The key to breaking free from these worries is to clearly recognize that any thoughts you have are nothing more than fresh delusions. By learning to observe your thoughts without immediately responding or getting caught up in them, you can gradually loosen their grip.

Don't Take Your Own Thoughts Too Seriously

If you're someone who constantly worries about how others see you, your first priority should be to stop overthinking—this is because the real culprit behind your anxiety is your habit of overanalyzing.

The first step is to understand that delusions have no limits. The mind can easily conjure up the worst possible scenarios. We all have shameful, cruel, even absurd ideas, things you would never dare share with anyone. Our minds generate these thoughts effortlessly, much like how dreams unfold.

In fact, the brain absorbs everything we see and hear as *reactive memories*. Everything you see, everything you hear—even things you're not consciously aware of—is actually being processed by your brain and stored as memories. (This often becomes clear when monks enter a deep meditative state during training—a highly advanced level of concentration.)

These fragmented memories can combine and create completely new, baseless delusions. At any time, our emotional state—whether we're angry, anxious or doubtful—can further twist reality and lead to false interpretations. In a Buddhist seminar I attended once, someone who got lost as a child mentioned how they had dreamed that their parents died in a tragic accident. Another person, scolded by their mother one night, had a nightmare that the mother tried to kill them with a knife.

It sounds ridiculous, but that's the nature of dreams and delusions—they distort things that have really happened.

Today, social media and mass media bombard us with countless triggers for desire, fear and insecurity. The information we absorb in the form of reactive memories shapes our subconscious, often resurfacing as unexpected anxieties.

But remember—these are all just delusions, nothing more.

The key is to be prepared. Recognize that delusions are just delusions. No matter what crosses your mind, don't take the bait.

Why not make a conscious decision right now about how you will handle these runaway thoughts?

"A thought is just a thought."

"There is no end to delusions, and they have no solid foundation."

"From this moment on, I refuse to chase after my own imagination."

Trust me: if you maintain this practice of not reacting, one day soon, you will feel truly free from others' opinions.

Let go of what you can't prove

While we're on the subject of recognizing that delusions are just delusions, it's worth keeping in mind that there is no way to verify a delusion.

When people have a wild thought or a dream, they tend to wonder, "Does this mean something important?" or "Did I see this for a reason?" It's human nature to search for meaning.

And sure, it *might* mean something. But what's crucial to understand is that there is simply no way to confirm that. The only way to try would be to dive headfirst into the world of speculation and blind belief. And the deeper you go, the further you drift from real understanding.

So, the question is this: Do you want to chase after delusions or do you want to stay grounded in reality? The way of thinking taught by the Buddha chooses the latter.

What separates this way of thinking from religion, mysticism, the occult, fortune-telling and even some schools of thought commonly lumped under the umbrella of "Buddhism" is simple: Does it seek meaning in the unprovable?

Many spiritual traditions treat unverifiable ideas as absolute truth. Religions do this. So do the occult and fortune-telling. Even within many so-called "Buddhist" teachings, you will find this tendency.

But the approach that most likely reflects the perspective of the historical Buddha is different. He made a conscious choice to leave unverifiable things out of the conversation entirely. And he was very clear about why:

> *Is the universe eternal, or will it end? Is it finite, or is it infinite? Do souls exist? Is there an afterlife? I do not claim to teach these things as truths.*
>
> *Why? Because they do not lead to clarity or peace of mind. They do not help free us from the suffering caused by desire.*
>
> *What I teach is this: insights that will help you achieve these goals.*
>
> *Life involves suffering. Suffering has a cause. Suffering can be ended. And there is a path to doing so. These are the Four Noble Truths.*
>
> —**"Teachings to the Disciple Malunkyaputta,"**
> ***The Middle-Length Discourses***

This thoroughly rational attitude is exactly what we need today. Whatever suffering we may be dealing with, we shouldn't react by chasing after unverifiable ideas like past lives or the afterlife. The essence of the Buddha's way of thinking is that such pursuits aren't necessary to alleviate suffering. How much you want to chase after the unprovable is up to you, but it is essential to have clarity on your purpose in life.

Buddhism's purpose is simple: to help us understand the true nature of our suffering so that we can free ourselves from it. To that end, it provides practical methods like meditation, including Zen and *vipassana*, and core mindsets like the cultivation of benevolence. When you put these into practice, they help you deal with real-world suffering. What more could you possibly need?

Chasing after delusion isn't necessary. What *is* necessary is understanding your own mind, learning to think clearly and gaining a rational grasp of reality. Since your suffering arises in this life, it can also be resolved in this life. Trust in that.

Keep Your Distance from Toxic People

If you're always worried about how others perceive you, there may be one particular person who's influencing you more than you realize. Often, when we say we feel watched or judged, what we really mean is that one specific person's gaze has gotten under our skin.

A woman once shared this frustration with me: "I find social interactions exhausting. Even when a friend calls to check in, I feel like screaming at them to leave me alone."

She grew up with an obsessively controlling mother. From childhood, her mother micromanaged everything—which friends she could have, which hobbies to pursue, what color clothes to wear, how to style her hair, even the order in which she arranged her books.

As a teenager, she tried to push back, but her mother would explode into fits of rage. Eventually, the girl gave up and endured it in silence. When she finally left home after university, she thought she was free.

But years later, she still carried an ever-present frustration. She felt constantly scrutinized, like her every move was being judged. Outwardly, she smiled and functioned well at work, but inside, resentment festered—"Everyone's so annoying," "I wish they would all just go away." She spent her weekends and holidays hiding under the covers, sleeping her days away. During those times, if a friend or her mum called, it would be enough to send her over the edge.

Her stress wasn't coming from work or relationships. The real cause was the lingering shadow of her mother's interference—the buried memories and unresolved anger.

Truly breaking free meant creating distance, even from her family, when their influence turned toxic.

If you can identify the person who is getting under your own skin, there are some strategies you can put in place to break the cycle of emotional triggers. Years of buried anxiety can vanish in an instant.

How to Break Free from Longstanding Emotional Burdens

In the case of the woman who felt suffocated by her mother's excessive interference, the real source of her suffering was the unresolved anger and memories tied to her mother's interference in her life. Small, unrelated events would trigger thoughts like, "This is so annoying," "Why won't people just leave me alone?" or "I wish everyone would disappear." With that in mind, three key strategies emerge to break free from longstanding emotional burdens. Let's take a look at each of them in turn.

Notice the reaction, but don't engage with it

If memories of her mother's interference resurface, the woman should consciously remind herself, "This is just a memory. Nothing more than a mental illusion." A useful technique here is verbal labeling, which we covered in chapter one (see "How to Observe Your Mind," p. 19). Try repeating "Memory, memory, memory" out loud to create distance from the reaction and weaken its grip.

She should also acknowledge her lingering anger by saying, "I still have anger inside me." Many people feel guilty or ashamed for holding resentment toward their parents, or else they blame themselves, but there is no need to do either. Simply recognizing, "Yes, this anger exists" is enough.

The key is to keep noticing. Think of it as observing a habit—an ingrained mental pattern. Each time the reaction surfaces, label it—then let it go.

Awareness is the first step toward releasing these emotions. Watch how these mental patterns play out and take note of them.

Shift your focus to physical sensations

Physical sensations belong to a different mental system than emotions or memories. Redirecting attention to bodily sensations can effectively reset the reaction cycle.

Think about how young children react. They might be crying one minute, but give them sweets or a fun distraction, and their mood changes instantly. Their minds stop reacting to an emotion and start reacting to a physical sensation.

Adults can use the same principle. When negative memories or emotions surface, shift your focus to your body—go for a walk, exercise, take a bath. In the case of the woman we've been discussing, hot yoga became her go-to method for grounding herself in the present.

Cut off the source of negative reactions

Family relationships often reinforce those mental formations we discussed in Chapter 1 because we interact in the same ways over and over again. We unconsciously fall into the same familiar roles—parent and child, caregiver and dependent—and repeat the same emotional patterns. Naturally, this means the same reactions emerge as well.

Ideally, the relationship will be positive and bring feelings of joy, but if it continually triggers negative reactions, it instead becomes a cycle of suffering. Some people even find that, no matter how stable they feel, visiting their childhood home brings out an old, unpleasant side of themselves, which they end up resenting themselves for.

If your interactions with someone—whether they're a family member or not—are prolonging your suffering, taking a step back from them is sometimes the best course of action. If their presence intensifies your mental formations, temporarily cutting off contact can be a wise decision. If you feel drained or anxious, put in place boundaries to gradually move away from that person rather than reacting in the moment. Choose distance over drama and remember that it's not your job to "fix" anyone.

> *Attachment gives rise to love. Love gives rise to suffering. Understanding that love can lead to hardship, walk alone like a rhinoceros.*
>
> —"The Rhinoceros," *The Collection of Discourses*

Some people hesitate to take this step, afraid that cutting someone off is too extreme. But creating distance can be a necessary reset, giving both sides the space to redefine their relationship. Ideally, you want to create some distance until you stop reacting to both the memories of the past and the person in the present.

Here, you might want to adopt a big-picture mindset. You can tell yourself, "Eventually, we will be able to understand each other" or "This is tough, but it will get sorted out sooner or later." The human heart is impermanent, and situations change over time. So, consider saying to yourself, "Let's take a step back for now."

In the woman's case, she made a firm decision: "I'm not going to contact my mother for a while." She spoke about it with a clear, refreshed sense of relief. "Once I get married, I'll reassess how I want to engage with her."

Stop Comparing—Focus on Your Own Path

Deep down, we all know that the best thing we can do to achieve happiness is to focus on ourselves, yet we can't help but look at others. We get distracted, lose sight of our own priorities and end up feeling frustrated. One of the biggest culprits is the tendency to compare ourselves to others.

The way out isn't to suppress these comparisons, but to notice them and choose not to react. Then, we can redirect our attention back to our own path. This isn't just wishful thinking—it's entirely possible. And if we take a page from the Buddha's book and think rationally, we can make it happen. But first, it's important to understand why we have this urge to compare.

Why comparisons are an irrational trap

We see an article listing the average salary for people our age, and we either breathe a sigh of relief or sink into self-doubt. We watch successful people in various industries and suddenly feel inadequate or anxious. Our minds are constantly scanning the world, collecting information about jobs, status, income, appearance, education and reputation—just to gauge where we stand.

What's really going on here?

At the root of comparison is that desire for validation that keeps cropping up. We want to feel reassured. We want to think, "I'm doing okay." Or, better yet, "I'm ahead." But if you were truly at peace with yourself—if you didn't crave external approval—would you even feel the need to compare?

Chances are, you compare because you're still struggling to fully accept yourself. You want proof of your worth. You want permission to say, "I'm good enough."

Here's the truth: comparisons are completely irrational. To begin with, they're based on delusion. Comparisons aren't rooted in anything real—they're just mental projection, a kind of daydream. That's why they never feel truly satisfying.

Secondly, they don't change your situation. No matter how much you compare, it won't improve your reality. This means that any sense of reassurance is fleeting at best.

Thirdly, it's an impossible game to win. To feel truly secure through comparison, you would have to be on top in every aspect of life. But let's face it—that's never going to happen. You're always going to have some lingering dissatisfaction.

When you look at it this way, comparison is not only irrational, but also a complete waste of time. So, why do we keep falling into this trap? Simply put, it's because we're used to it.

Delusions are easy. They require no effort. They're habits we've indulged in for so long that they feel like second nature. Reality might be tough to change, but a quick mental comparison? That's always within reach. And when we land on the "I'm better" side of the equation, we get a temporary ego boost.

At the end of the day, however, comparison is just another way to kill time. It's nothing more than a distraction.

> *The wise understand that when a person sees their own achievements as superior and others' as inferior, they create attachment—attachment that leads to suffering.*
>
> *Do not think of yourself as equal, superior or inferior to others. Any of these thoughts will lead only to more suffering.*
>
> —"The Supreme Thought," *The Collection of Discourses*

The Right Kind of Effort

If comparison is just a destructive mental habit, then the smart move is to cut it off at the root. Why waste time on something so pointless when you could be focusing on what really matters?

If you crave validation, fine—but channel it in the right direction. Here's how:

1. Use your desire for recognition as motivation to improve your work and daily life.
2. Focus on your own path, no matter what others are doing.
3. Let your own sense of fulfillment be your guide.

We've seen that, unless you're planning to become a monk, there's no need to suppress your desire for recognition. Whether it's the urge not to lose to your rivals, the need to protect your pride by winning, the ambition to achieve results that earn you appreciation or the drive to sharpen your skills even further—if these motivations fuel your activities, then go all out and give it your best shot!

But always remember: validation can be a motivation, but it should never be your goal.

Why? Because external recognition is ultimately outside your control. If you make it your goal, you will end up obsessing over what others think—and placing your happiness in the hands of others like this is the road to misery.

Success, recognition and approval—these are external factors, future outcomes, things you can't dictate. The only things within your control are your own thoughts, your own actions and the present moment. Everything else is ultimately just delusion—and you know now that, in the Buddha's teachings, delusions are never meant to be the goal.

Wanting to be recognized is a great starting motivation or a direction to aim for when you set out. But once you get going, it's time to switch gears to a more Buddhist mindset—think *improvement* and *focus*.

Improvement

In work, in daily life or in any new endeavor, I encourage adopting a mindset of continuous improvement.

In Buddhist terms, improvement means *creating conditions that bring a sense of ease.* This could mean refining your workflow, upgrading your tools, changing your environment, adjusting your habits, updating your computer software, tweaking little things like lighting, playing background music and even adjusting your social interactions. The goal is simple: make things feel right so you can stay engaged with them.

Your mind constantly evaluates everything in two ways: *pleasant* or *unpleasant.* When something feels unpleasant, your mind wants to escape—that's stress. On the other hand, when something feels pleasant, your mind wants to stay—that's motivation. But here's the key: even as you improve your conditions, practice not reacting to every discomfort or pleasure that arises. Steadiness is what allows improvement to serve you, rather than control you. Have fun with it!

Focus

Focus isn't about aiming for external things like being recognized by others or achieving results. No matter what your initial motivation is, once you get started, it's important to focus on your internal motivations. In other words, cherish the sense of joy that comes from concentration and fulfillment, and keep pushing through on a single task.

In Zen monasteries, monks engage in *samu*—physical labor done with full mindfulness. They don't question whether it's meaningful or not. They just do it, fully present, taking satisfaction in the work itself. That is the mindset we should adopt.

THE ZEN ART OF FOCUSING ON YOUR OWN PATH

"Your own path" refers to the work that truly matters to you—things that are useful, necessary and can be done with just your own effort. What others think or what the people around you are doing has nothing to do with it.

Real effort means noticing distractions—other people's opinions, comparisons or expectations—and choosing not to react to them. It's about fully focusing on your own work and being at peace with the process. This is what leads to real results.

Let's break down the steps to mastering this focus, guided by Zen wisdom:

The first step is to close your eyes. This is a fundamental wellness practice—one that should be at the core of your daily life.

As we've explored, the mind reacts to everything it encounters. It's not as strong as you might think. The moment you step outside, it reacts. The moment you see someone, it reacts. And with each reaction, your mind accumulates noise and clutter. That's just how it works. We tend to let ourselves get too caught up in the outside world. We're constantly distracted, our minds are restless and unsettled.

So, what's the best solution? Simple—don't look. Don't let your mind be hijacked by external distractions. Just close your eyes.

Once your eyes are shut, turn your attention inward. This is where your real work begins.

The second step is to reset unnecessary reactions.

Now that your eyes are closed, shift your focus to the state of your mind. You might notice exhaustion, stress, frustration, tension or just a cloud of vague, restless thoughts floating around. That's fine. Whatever is there, just acknowledge it as it is. Observe it objectively, like a neutral third party.

Spend 30 seconds, maybe 5 minutes—whatever feels right for you—just watching your mind. If you're feeling especially unsettled, I recommend setting a timer for 15 minutes.

Simply by doing this, your mind will begin to clear. Unnecessary reactions will fade, and your thoughts will settle into a calm, steady state. This is how you reset.

The third step is to open your eyes and get to work.

Once your time is up, open your eyes wide and dive into your task with full focus. That initial burst of momentum is crucial. After resetting, launch into action with everything you've got.

Your concentration will naturally fade after a while—that's normal. When that happens, take a short break, go back to the first step and restart the process.

This simple three-step method is a practical, everyday version of what the Buddha called the "Noble Eightfold Path": a roadmap for achieving fulfillment.

Three key principles from the Eightfold Path are at play here—*right mindfulness* (being fully aware of the present moment), *right concentration* (focusing completely on one thing) and *right effort* (sustaining awareness and concentration over time). The practice of Zen and *vipassana* meditation is all about fully activating this trio of elements to reach a state of ultra-high concentration known as *meditative concentration* (*jhanasamadhi*). But you don't have to be a monk to use this method. It works just as well in daily life. That's exactly why I've laid out these three steps. You can apply them at work, at home—anywhere. I encourage you to put them into practice.

Try it out. Close your eyes, calm your mind and, when you're ready, declare, "Let's begin!" (In Zen practice, we often say "Decision!," or "*Kettei!*")

Just like a long-jumper builds momentum before leaping, use these three steps to propel yourself forward. See how far you can go.

WORK WITH A CLEAR MIND

Once you've started a task, don't let yourself get distracted by what others might think or what's happening in the world around you.

When you tackle something, do it with a commitment to *no-mindedness* or *non-thought* (*acitta*). The principle is to focus all your heart and energy on one thing at a time.

By doing so, unnecessary mental noise will dissolve, and your mind will become sharper, clearer and more focused. You will feel a deep sense of satisfaction—because true fulfillment comes from effort that you believe in.

Once you've mastered this kind of effort, outside validation becomes meaningless. When you focus, success naturally follows and, along the way, you might even receive gratitude or recognition from others. But at that point, it won't really matter to you.

Why? Because when you're satisfied with the journey itself—the process of tackling your own challenges—those things will start to seem irrelevant.

You know what needs to be done. Reset, focus and give it your best. That's it. Once you've accomplished it, you will feel a sense of satisfaction, and that's all it takes to wrap things up nicely.

Doesn't worrying about what others think seem irrelevant now?

As the Buddha taught, when we live authentically and free ourselves from other people's opinions, we release ourselves from the reactive patterns that are keeping us stuck and the answers naturally reveal themselves.

Never abandon your own path to chase someone else's.
Know your own work. Devote yourself fully to it.

—"On the Self," *The Path of the Dhamma*

Now that we've learned how to change our mindset to avoid comparison with others, let's look at how we can develop the right motivation to engage with the world.

CHAPTER 5

COMPETING THE RIGHT WAY

Is the Competition Just an Illusion?

COMPETITION IS AN unavoidable part of life. People tend to react to the world around them, letting their desires get the better of them—the urge to win, the need to keep up appearances and the pull of their own pride. No matter where you go, you will find yourself in some kind of race—whether it's for a promotion, social status or just proving your worth. But with competition comes anxiety, stress and the overwhelming pressure to win. Losing brings feelings of defeat and inferiority. It's no wonder competition weighs so heavily on our minds.

To navigate this, it helps to understand what competition truly is—and to learn ways of engaging with it that minimize unnecessary suffering.

Understanding the Mechanics of Competition

What exactly is competition? If we analyze it through the Buddhist lens of observing the mind, we see that competition once again stems from desire—the craving to obtain something.

All living beings are wired to chase after what they believe will satisfy them. It's a basic survival instinct, embedded in our brains. But for humans, satisfaction isn't limited to the essentials we need for survival, like food, shelter or clothing. We also crave symbols of validation: status, brands, academic achievements, physical appearance, career success. These symbols, however, are finite. When multiple people seek the same thing, struggle ensues, and the one who secures the prize is deemed the winner. Thus, competition is born.

But it doesn't stop there. Humans are inherently greedy. We don't just want to win the thing itself, we want to be *better* than others. We chase higher ranks, greater influence and bigger rewards. And because greed never knows when to call it quits, no matter how many symbols we accumulate, we find ourselves stuck in an endless loop—constantly competing for the next big thing.

The thirst for recognition also fuels this cycle. We want to be valued, admired and validated, so we react to these cravings by pushing ourselves harder, believing that each victory will bring us closer to fulfillment.

At the root of competition, then, are two conflicting forces: the primitive belief that obtaining something will satisfy us, and the reality that nothing is ever enough. As long as these forces drive us, we're automatically pulled into an endless race.

> *People are never truly satisfied. Their hearts are driven by thirsting desire, always chasing after something more.*
>
> —**"On Those Who Renounce Covetousness,"** ***The Connected Discourses***

The misconception that "victory tastes sweet"

Competition isn't just fueled by our own personal desire to win—society itself imposes it on us.

In nearly every aspect of life, we're pitted against each other—companies fight for market dominance, professionals compete for promotions, and even children, once they grow out of fighting over toys, measure their worth by their grades and popularity.

What you will find, however, is that many of these competitions are artificial constructs designed to serve someone else's interests. Without even realizing it, we unwittingly get sucked into these virtual competitions, believing they matter. This leads to an endless stream of unnecessary reactions. We reproach ourselves, asking "Why am I not good enough? Why haven't I achieved more?"

One of the clearest examples of this can be found in the education system.

We've all been through it—kids, as they grow, start caring a lot about their self-worth. By the time they hit middle school, puberty kicks in and, suddenly, grades matter because their report cards affect their future. They begin to obsess over their academic performance.

In reality, if we look at the true essence of studying—gaining intellectual ability—there are more important things to focus on than just celebrating or agonizing over test results. But the adults around them—parents, teachers and tutors—keep pushing a different narrative: "Look, here are your grades, your ranking, your percentile!" They hand kids a measuring stick to assess their worth.

Until this point, most children never even think about measuring their worth. But now, they learn to gauge their value based on grades and rankings. They start constructing a mindset:

1. I want to be recognized.
2. To be recognized, I need better grades.
3. Therefore, improving my grades becomes my goal.

But deep down, many kids—probably including you, once upon a time—question this system. The truth is, *improving grades* is an entirely arbitrary goal, something without real substance.

Children who ask "Why do I even have to study?" instinctively sense that school learning is just an abstract concept, a collection of symbols and illusions. It's not particularly fun to them, nor does it fulfill their curiosity. There is no *joy* in it, so sticking with it feels unnatural to the heart.

Yet, children also have the desire to be acknowledged. That single desire drives them to accept the idea that their worth is defined by their grades. Since all the adults around them seem to operate under this belief, they start to buy into the illusion that grades, rankings and academic success are absolute measures of worth.

If a child were enlightened like the Buddha, they might walk alone, "like a rhinoceros," unaffected by the competition. But most children, longing for approval from adults, charge ahead "like a wild boar," diving headfirst into the academic contest. And before they know it, they're caught up in the competition, running a race they never signed up for.

What creates competition is nothing more than a value system—a judgment, a mere illusion. It's built on the mistaken idea that test results have inherent value, a misunderstanding passed down by adults.

For some schools and academies, boosting students' test results is their business model—it's how they make a profit or increase their profile.

Parents, on the other hand, find their own sense of pride (or desire for validation) in their child's academic success. Some even use their child's achievements to compensate for their own past failures, vicariously seeking victories they missed out on when they were children, as we saw in the mother and daughter anecdote in Chapter 2.

And then there are the children themselves. They come to see studying as a competition to win. If they score highly, they believe people will think they're smart, and that protects their pride.

Everyone has their own "honey"—the sweet satisfaction of getting what they want—which is why they willingly engage in pointless academic competition with their peers. People can't escape their illusions, so they remain trapped by their attachment to the symbols of grades and rankings.

There are no perfect winners

I was once caught in this virtual competition myself. It was a world where people clung to their pride, desperately using academics to defend their self-worth.

In that world, no one is ever truly satisfied. The game never ends—you're always chasing the next prestigious title, the next achievement that might keep your pride intact. Every academic decision—what field of study to choose, what career path to take—is driven by this need to "win" in the competition. Even decades later, after retirement, some people still can't let go of their obsession with pride.

Once you get on this virtual competition ride, you can't

easily get off. "Good grades," "being smart," "winning," "pride"—these are nothing more than delusions created by the need for validation. But stepping off the ride feels like losing, and no one wants to be seen as a loser. So people keep running, determined never to fall behind.

The people trapped in this world always seem anxious, afraid of judgment and perpetually thirsty for approval.

> *This world is consumed by battles, disputes, worries, grief, greed, arrogance and slander.*
> *In the end, all things led to loss, and I was left feeling empty.*
>
> —**"Struggle" and "Weapons,"** ***The Collection of Discourses***

There is no denying that competition exists in reality. Losing can sometimes have real consequences, so the desire to win makes sense. But if you only fixate on the virtual feeling of winning, you get stuck in an endless loop of competition. True victory—the kind that brings peace—never actually exists. Most people will experience losing at some point and, unless they shift their mindset, that pain will haunt them for a lifetime.

Buddhism doesn't say deny reality or drop out of competition, nor does it advocate for blindly conforming. Instead, it asks *how* you will face reality. It urges you to establish your own approach, rooted in calm observation rather than compulsive response.

Prepare Yourself Before Stepping into Competition

When it comes to dealing with competition, most people consider two options:

1. Join the race and aim to win, accepting that this is just how the world works.
2. Step away from competition and seek a different way of life.

Either you play the game or you opt out—that's the common way of thinking.

There are plenty of self-help messages out there preaching so-called philosophies of winning and success or, on the flip side, urging people to quit the rat race and live freely. Many assume Buddhism aligns with the second idea—walking away from competition.

If we really push deeper into the Buddha's way of thinking, however, we find there is actually another, much deeper question to ask: What kind of mindset will I choose to face reality with? In other words, instead of rejecting competition, we focus on how to exist within it—on what kind of mindset we maintain while engaging with the world.

From there, a third option emerges:

3. Move through competition with a different motivation.

This means living within a competitive society, but not being driven solely by the need to win. Instead of getting caught up in the black-and-white thinking of winning or losing, you embrace a completely different value system for yourself.

A Zen monk's advice: "Close your eyes and see"

Living in a competitive world with a different set of motivations and values—can that really be done? The Buddha's way of thinking says yes.

To do that, however, you first need to step outside the illusion of competition for a moment and focus on your own path. Here's a simple way to do just that.

One day, a person exhausted by "the rat race" visited a Zen temple and spoke of their struggles. The monk listened and said, "Close your eyes and see."

Let's try it now. When you close your eyes, what do you see? Darkness, no doubt. In that darkness, there are no rankings, no rivals, no society to judge you. The world as we know it doesn't exist.

What you see in that darkness are your own thoughts—take a good look at what comes floating up.

"I refuse to lose."

"I'm going to win."

"I'm going to make people acknowledge me."

"I don't want to be looked down on. I can't stand being made light of."

Perhaps these are the kinds of thoughts that start bubbling up?

The desire for victory, pride, self-esteem, vanity and the need to show off—all of these feelings spring from the darkness within our own hearts. Thoughts like being left behind, feeling inferior, losing or questioning our own worth also emerge from the same shadowy place.

Take a moment to truly recognize the principle at work here. First, there is a craving. Second, there is a desire to win. And third, there is an automatic reaction—a mindset driven by the judgment of winning or losing, a tendency to compare yourself to others and a competitive spirit.

And now, understand this—just as we've seen in previous chapters, all of those thoughts are delusions.

Wanting to win, feeling victorious, hating to lose, feeling defeated—these are all delusions. See them for what they are. Such is the true essence of competition.

Now, open your eyes. Take a good look at what's in front of you. It can be the scene inside the room or the view outside; either one is fine.

What do you see? Light. Color. Reality. The delusions that were floating in your mind just a moment ago are nowhere to be found, no matter where you look.

You may ask yourself, "So that was all just an illusion?" Realize this truth, and feel it deeply.

The things we usually take as real—social values that pit us against each other in terms of winning and losing or success and failure—are, in a strict sense, nothing more than illusions. They drift through our minds, whispering, "Win, achieve, don't fall behind." Without realizing it, we live under their spell. It's no different from being caught inside a dream.

"But even if I understand this," you might say, "I still have to return to reality. Won't I just get caught up in competition again?" No. And this is a crucial insight in Buddhist thought. The real question isn't about external reality—it's about your internal reality. How are you facing competition? What kind of mindset do you carry each day?

External circumstances are secondary. The competition itself is just a background detail. More importantly, you should work to become aware of your own mind—of how you respond, how you think, how you feel. It's essential to understand what mindset we have when confronting the outside world.

Close your eyes, and all that remains is the illusion created by your own desires. Recognize this, and take the first step toward freeing yourself from competition.

If the Buddha Were Here, He Would Say, "Wake Up!"

Those who can see don't need to look. Those who can hear don't need to listen.

The wise walk through this world as if they know nothing at all.

—"Elder Kaccayana," *The Verses of the Elder Monks*

People tend to chase after symbols of victory—things like money, status, reputation, academic achievements, brand names and more. But no matter how much they win, their minds are never truly at peace. Even when they think, "I did it!" or "I won!," there are always more lingering thoughts—"I don't want to lose to anyone" or "I need to win more."

On the flip side, if you think of the competition as a loss, your heart will forever be haunted by regrets, chasing after victories that slipped away. Even as the years go by and the rivalry feels like a distant memory, you might find yourself daydreaming, wondering, "If I had done this back then, maybe I could have won" or "If I really put in the effort now, could I still come out on top?" People live their whole lives like sleepwalkers, aimlessly drifting through the fog of wanting to win.

If the Buddha were here, he would say, "Wake up!" He would ask, "Do you really think you should go through life along this path that leaves you unfulfilled?"

Competition is a real part of society, and it's certainly possible to strive for victory. Striving to win can sometimes bring not just personal satisfaction but also happiness to others in unexpected ways.

However, how you choose to face the reality of competition is up to you.

The important thing is to pull yourself out of the virtual competition—the imaginary race happening entirely in your own head. Take a step back and wake up from this illusion. Only then do you gain real choices. Will you stay in the race? Jump out of it? Or will you find a new motivation to live by? True victory—the kind that brings deep satisfaction—only becomes possible after you have done that.

If you're constantly worried about what others think, close your eyes.

If you're struggling under the weight of people judging winners and losers, open your eyes.

Closing your eyes helps you stop reacting. Opening your eyes helps you see through delusion. It's simple, but this is the first step to breaking free from the mental trap of competition.

Try it. Reclaim your inner freedom.

Those who react to the outside world without looking within themselves are easily swept away by desire.

Those who clearly see both the world and their own hearts remain free, untouched by illusion.

—"The Confession of Rakkhita," *The Verses of the Elder Monks*

The Four Mindsets for Harmonious Relationships

A key teaching from the Buddha—one that shapes how we can live within the competitive world without being consumed by reactions to it—revolves around the four essential mindsets of *loving-kindness*, *compassion*, *sympathetic joy* and *equanimity*.

These qualities train us to respond to experiences—and to people—without being swept away by automatic reactions. Cultivating them helps us maintain calm observation, even in situations that would normally trigger emotions like stress, anger or envy.

Loving-kindness is the sincere wish for others to be happy. It's not about personal gain or control. It's simply wanting happiness for others, with no strings attached.

Compassion is the ability to truly understand and empathize with another person's suffering.

Sympathetic joy means wholeheartedly sharing in someone else's happiness and success, empathizing with their joy.

Equanimity is the ability to let go, to remain steady and unaffected by emotional turbulence. It's about recognizing when desires, anger or attachment take hold and consciously choosing not to react impulsively.

In everyday language, people often lump these together as *love*. But the term *love* is vague and, at times, *love* can inadvertently lead us to suffering. Buddhism breaks it down into these four distinct forces of the heart, offering a clearer and more practical approach.

Everyone possesses these four mindsets to some degree.

We all want our family and loved ones to be happy. We all hope that those close to us will live fulfilling lives. This is loving-kindness.

When you see someone struggling, you feel their pain and want to help. When you hear about people in far-off countries facing disasters like earthquakes, you naturally want to support them. This is compassion.

Watching your pet settle down for a cozy nap brings you a sense of calm and peace, or seeing a child laugh in the park fills you with warmth. This is sympathetic joy.

You can choose to forgive or let go of past resentment. You can strive not to react in order to curtail suffering. This is equanimity.

The last of these, equanimity, may well be the hardest to cultivate, and that is because of our attachments—to satisfying our desires, to holding on to grudges, to winning, to being right and to getting what we want. We justify these attachments by telling ourselves, "It's for their own good," "It's for justice" or even "It's for love." This holds true whether in something as intimate as a parent–child relationship or something as abstract as international relations. But in Buddhist thought, these are just labels. The real challenge is to closely examine the emotions driving us. Are we responding to the events in our lives with clarity or are we just automatically reacting?

Seeing ourselves clearly is the essence of the Buddha's way of thinking.

Building the foundation for a life you can say yes to

The four mindsets of loving-kindness, compassion, sympathetic joy and equanimity are at the heart of the practice of not reacting. Unfortunately, however, modern society rarely teaches us about them. These aren't religious or ideological concepts, but universal ways of engaging our hearts that everyone inherently holds—and yet, so many people go through life unaware of them.

As a result, many of us spend our years reacting haphazardly with desire, anger and delusions, and find ourselves stuck in a cycle of frustration and disappointment. We lash out at family members without realizing the hurt we cause. We chase career success at the expense of others. When alone, we obsess over competition, our pride and our self-worth. Even indulgences and pleasure fail to satisfy us, leaving us restless, anxious about the future or haunted by the past. At some point, we might ask ourselves, "Is this really how I want to live?"

We realize our heart feels parched. We're anxious. But we just don't know what to do. Such is the tough reality we find ourselves in.

Is there a way to hit the reset button on a life that feels lost and directionless? Can we live in a way that allows us to say to ourselves, "Yes, this feels right"—a way that brings us real satisfaction?

What the Buddha taught was that in order to understand your own mind, you need to recognize your reactions and act from the right motivation. That means grounding yourself in the four essential mindsets and making them the foundation of your life's motivation.

Find the right motivation

As we have seen, we all have three choices: jump into the competition, step away from it or navigate it with a different motivation. But what does this *different motivation* look like? Let me share a story.

I once knew a man who worked for a prestigious international consulting firm. Highly educated and making an impressive salary, he was what society calls an *elite*. But his workplace was brutal—rampant backstabbing, cut-throat competition and colleagues secretly rejoicing when someone else failed, fell ill or got demoted. It was a toxic battlefield.

This man was suffering from chronic stress to the point that he relied on pain medication just to get through the day. "If I keep this up, I'm going to burn out completely. Maybe I should just quit," he told me.

What I suggested was this: "Try looking at your colleagues with a compassionate heart." In an environment driven by ruthless competition, if you react out of pure self-interest—thinking, "I have to win! I can't afford to lose!"—your heart will soon be consumed with anger. Sure, quitting is one option. But before making that decision, there is something else to try: anchor yourself in the right motivation.

The right motivation comes from compassion. Chances are, most of the people in his office had probably never experienced true peace. They were constantly being pushed by their own ambition, pride and vanity, working as if their lives depended on it. Many were consumed by stress, exhaustion, paranoia and hostility. A heart devoid of joy is a hollow one. Some of them were probably wondering, "Why am I even doing this?"

The first step for this man was to acknowledge his colleagues' suffering and to understand it—to look at them and think, "*Everyone is doing their best.*"

If you, too, can bring yourself to see this in the people around you, the world starts to look different. When we are trapped by desire, our world feels small, but when we come from a place of compassion, we start to feel connected. The world suddenly seems bigger, more open.

The power of loving-kindness, compassion, sympathetic joy and equanimity

To live is to be marked by suffering—so teaches the first of the Buddha's Four Noble Truths, which we met in Chapter 1. Some people hear this and think Buddhism is pessimistic and depressing, but that isn't the case. This teaching isn't negative—it's simply acknowledging a fact of life that we all experience.

"Life isn't easy." That's not a complaint—it's a statement of how things are.

Importantly, this truth isn't the conclusion we should draw about life. It's the starting point—the place from which we begin to build a life free from suffering.

The Buddha's message is one of hope: "You can rise above suffering."

There is another essential truth from the Buddha's teachings: "You're not alone. Everyone carries their own burdens."

Every single person—your family, your colleagues, the strangers packed into the morning train, the people you pass on the street, even the celebrities on TV—each of them carries their own struggles and pain. When you open your eyes to this truth, something shifts. Your own suffering might feel a little lighter. That crushing sense of loneliness might begin to melt away, even if just a little bit.

The moment we recognize that *everyone* is doing their best to survive their own reality, we take the first step toward a new way of living. That's the power of compassion—it transforms how we see the world.

The man from earlier told me that simply learning about these four mindsets—loving-kindness, compassion, sympathetic joy and equanimity—helped him feel calmer. After that, his workplace didn't seem quite as unbearable anymore. Simply by understanding how to approach life differently, he began to change the ways he reacted. That's why it's so valuable to learn from different philosophies, spiritual traditions and perspectives—not just Buddhism. New insights can give us hope and direction. They are always a worthy pursuit.

"If I Can Be of Help, That's Enough"

When we make these four mindsets the foundation of our lives, our perspective on work and purpose shifts.

Loving-kindness is the desire for others to be happy and well. From there, wanting to help people follows naturally.

We think: "What matters most is contributing to others. If I can be of service, that's enough."

When your heart is filled with sympathetic joy, we find happiness in seeing others happy. The more we recognize and consciously appreciate the joy of others, the more we can react to it and experience it for ourselves.

Compassion allows us to readily see other people's pain. It helps us instinctively understand that causing harm or inflicting suffering on others is something we should avoid at all costs.

To contribute, to serve, to bring happiness to others—these are the natural expressions of loving-kindness, compassion and sympathetic joy. When we live by these principles, isn't that already enough to give life meaning?

The more we cling to our cravings—our selfish desires, anger and delusions—the more suffering we create for ourselves. We chase after things with the thought of winning or getting what we want, imagining a future where we've achieved it.

But desire is nothing more than a mix of craving and delusion. The moment we start chasing after it, we lose sight of ourselves, forgetting our true way of living and what really leads to a positive state of mind. So many people have lost their way like this.

That is why the Buddha urges us to wake up: "Observe your own reactions. Be aware of them. And let go of the reactions that cause suffering. Free yourself."

Loving-kindness, compassion, sympathetic joy and equanimity are easy to forget in the chaos of life, but they are timeless truths, and they are essential for true happiness.

If we make these four mindsets the foundation of our purpose for living, we can free ourselves—even if just a little—from the cycle of greed, anger and delusion.

When that happens, we discover that even in the midst of competition, we don't have to suffer.

Beware of the Five Hindrances

The Buddha taught that, in our journey toward fulfillment and adopting the four mindsets, we must be mindful not to react to their antitheses—the "Five Hindrances":

> *Traveler on the path, become aware of the turmoil within your own mind. There, you will find five obstacles: indulgence in pleasure, anger, lack of motivation, restless distraction and doubt.*
>
> *Recognize this: in such a state of mind, understanding is clouded and clear thinking is impossible. Thus, the cycle of suffering will persist indefinitely.*
>
> —"Instructions for Young Ascetics," *The Middle-Length Discourses*

These Five Hindrances are always present within us. When things go wrong, when we fail, when we hit a wall, one or more of these hindrances are usually the cause. That's why the Buddha warned us to remain vigilant.

Let's take a closer look at these Five Hindrances and how they manifest.

A checklist of what holds you back in life

Indulgence in pleasure refers to the tendency to chase sensory pleasures—sights, sounds, smells, tastes and physical sensations. TV, books, social media, gourmet food and countless other forms of entertainment fall under this category. Enjoying these in moderation is fine, but if you find yourself compulsively reaching for distractions, losing hours to entertainment or unable to control your impulses, then enjoying these pleasures may have turned into a hindrance. It's something that needs to be addressed.

Anger includes frustration, dissatisfaction, sadness, stress and resentment toward others. When anger takes hold, our thoughts become clouded and productivity plummets.

Some argue that anger fuels motivation, but, from a Buddhist perspective, that's a dangerous misconception. Those who rely on anger as an incentive will find themselves constantly triggered, reacting emotionally rather than thinking clearly. Over time, they usually accumulate more failures than successes because of their unchecked temper.

Motivation is meant to lead you into a state of focus

without unnecessary reactions. However, anger *is* a reaction. Between a state where there are no unnecessary reactions in your mind versus one where you have an angry reaction, which do you think allows you to perform better? As we've seen, true motivation comes from a state of calm focus, not an emotional outburst. This should be an important principle when aiming for success.

Lack of motivation is when you feel tired, lazy or uninterested, when you cut corners and want to give up on your endeavors. These states sap your energy and prevent progress.

The reasons for a lack of motivation can be difficult to pin down. However, for instance, if you find that even after resting, your motivation hasn't returned, it might be that you're chasing the wrong kind of goal or that perhaps the tasks themselves or your relationships aren't bringing you pleasure. Building on the ideas in Chapters 3 and 4 about valuing pleasure and continual improvements, I would like to encourage you to get creative with your daily life.

Restless distraction refers to a scattered mind, overwhelmed with random thoughts and delusions, which struggles to focus. This state of affairs might be a result of getting too accustomed to the distractions of TV, the internet, video games or music, as well as the casual automatic reactions triggered by things like alcohol, tobacco and smartphones.

To counteract this, try reducing the number of unnecessary things that stimulate your mind. Take walks, disconnect from digital noise and practice mindfulness techniques such as Zen or *vipassana* meditation.

Doubt manifests as questioning yourself, mistrust in others or anxiety about the future. Thoughts like "What if I fail?," "I can't do this," "What if they don't like me?" or "What if I'm being deceived?" all stem from this hindrance, as do fears about the future.

From a Buddhist perspective, doubt is considered another form of delusion. The antidote lies in practicing mindfulness (*sati*), learning to recognize these thoughts as mere delusions and letting them go.

Turning your days around: Overcoming the Five Hindrances

The tricky thing about the Five Hindrances is just how powerful they are. You probably know what I mean—when you catch yourself thinking, "I know I shouldn't, but I just can't stop." However, the more you let these hindrances win, the more they chip away at you. Self-loathing creeps in and your confidence takes a hit.

At some point, if you want to turn things around, you *have* to overcome these Five Hindrances. So, how do you do it?

The mindset of the Buddha that we've explored in this

book is, in itself, the key to winning. For example, when a hindrance strikes, the best response is not to react impulsively but instead to simply acknowledge it.

Another strategy is to focus on your direction. Keep your goals in sight and remind yourself, "I can't let this take me down." Sometimes, just rallying your inner strength is enough to push through.

Additionally, there are two other valuable habits to develop: not using reactions as an escape and actively seeking enjoyment in the process.

STOP ESCAPING INTO REACTIONS

This means resisting those little urges—like flicking on the TV or scrolling the internet the second you have a free moment. In Buddhism, these tiny automatic reactions are called *leaks*. Your energy seeps out through small mental holes, leaving you unable to stay focused on what truly matters. Here's the thing: when these leaks add up, your chances of success drift further and further away.

Now, if your *only* goal is to relax and enjoy life, there's no harm done. But if you have anything important in your life that you need to accomplish—if there is a result you're determined to achieve—you will want to start making a rule for yourself: no escaping into mindless reactions. When you feel the impulse, resist it.

Instead, train yourself to pause and feel. Take a moment

to be still and notice your breath moving in and out. It might feel boring at first, but if it does, try setting a simple goal—become comfortable with just being still.

FIND ENJOYMENT IN THE PROCESS

This means making a deliberate effort to enjoy your work and daily tasks. It's about consciously choosing to react with enthusiasm—telling yourself, "This is fun."

In a way, this approach is the opposite of what we've discussed so far. Up until now, we've focused on not reacting—especially to negative impulses like desire, anger or distraction. However, it *can* be a good idea to consciously tap into those positive reactions that lift your spirits. Give yourself a little nudge with thoughts like, "This is interesting!" or "I'm really doing my best at this!"

The more you train your mind to engage positively, the more you shift from a dull, foggy mindset to a clearer, more enjoyable one. Over time, the Five Hindrances will lose their grip, allowing you to stay more focused and motivated.

Remember: joyful reactions don't just happen; they can be created through the right mindset.

Right effort minus the Five Hindrances equals life

There is one more thing you should understand about the Five Hindrances: your life is defined by what remains after subtracting them. The real you is what's left after you take away these distractions and weaknesses.

Sometimes, I meet people who say things like, "My life has been one failure after another" or "I can't even hold down a decent job." They sound ashamed. But when I ask them about their goals, they're full of ambition—"I want to succeed," "I want to be good at what I do." On the surface, they seem motivated.

Yet when you look at these people's daily lives, you can't help but find patterns—giving in to pleasure, choosing the easy way out, getting frustrated and quitting over small setbacks. Deep down, they can't accept these weaknesses. They inflate their egos. They cling to the belief that "they should be capable of more." They refuse to let go of the idea that "they're better than how they are."

In Buddhism, we're taught to see these weaknesses for what they are, without judgment.

As human beings, we all have our weak moments. Everyone makes compromises. Sometimes, we get lazy or we find ourselves chasing pleasure. Denying this reality won't change it. The real you is what remains after subtracting your moments of weakness, after filtering out the Five Hindrances.

This *true-to-size* version of yourself isn't something you can judge as good or bad—it simply is. It's the only real version of you, because everything else is just a fantasy.

The *better version of yourself* you imagine exists only within your own delusions. And the more you chase after it, the more miserable you will feel.

The *real* you is already there. You just need to accept yourself as the person you are now.

You are always at the starting line of your life. If you're not satisfied with where you are, then the path forward is simple: grow, improve and elevate yourself from this point on. As you do, don't let the Five Hindrances hold you back. This time, let's make sure you reach your true potential.

At its core, life is just this—the right kind of effort, minus the Five Hindrances. Whatever remains after that is your greatest result, your highest truth.

So, the challenge is, how much of your best self can you put forward? How much of your truest, strongest self can you bring to life?

And in the end, no matter where you land, make peace with it. Accept yourself—unconditionally. There's no need for justification, no need for reasons.

Freeing Yourself from the Fear of Losing

The stronger your desire to win, the harder it is to deal with loss. That's why, no matter how much times passes, so many people stay trapped—haunted by disappointment, crushed by setbacks, unable to escape the weight of failure. But we've seen how Buddhism teaches us that, ultimately, there is no such thing as winning and losing. Both are nothing more than delusions—fantasies created by desire and ego.

This isn't just some comforting thought. Once you really understand your own mind, this truth hits home in a way that's impossible to ignore—and, in that moment, you gain the ability to observe setbacks without being swept away by them.

The Trouble with Envy in the Present and Insecurities from the Past

Let's talk about envy for a moment. When we feel envious or jealous, it's because we're reacting to someone who seems to have more than us—someone who appears more talented, more successful or simply luckier. Whether it's feeling jealous of a well-respected colleague or getting anxious when we see people our age thriving, envy is always a reaction to someone else's situation.

Envy is a *present-tense* emotion. But once the outcome is settled—once we've "lost"—it shifts into *past-tense* feelings like insecurity, a lingering sense of inadequacy or even resentment. Either way, envy makes us suffer.

So, how do we break free? The answer lies in adopting the right mindset.

If we look at envy as *attachment*—a fixation on someone else—it opens the way to an important insight. Once we see it for what it is, we can notice the feeling without reacting to it, loosening its hold on us.

The Buddha once described three types of attachment that cause suffering:

1. *The attachment to wanting to obtain something but not getting it.*
2. *The attachment to holding on to what we have but eventually losing it.*
3. *The attachment to getting rid of what we don't want without being able to.*

—"The Buddha's First Teaching at Sarnath,"
The Connected Discourses

Envy is driven by two of these attachments. The first is the craving for self-recognition (the attachment to wanting to obtain something but not getting it). This stems from the desire for approval that we explored in Chapter 1. The second is the desire for your perceived rival to disappear (the attachment to getting rid of what we don't want without being able to). This reflects a state of anger directed toward that person.

In other words, the true nature of envy is the anger we direct at others when our need for validation is not fulfilled. It is, ultimately, one of the Three Poisons—greed, anger and delusion—that drive our suffering.

It's important to remember that this envy-driven anger

isn't actually caused by the other person. Think about it—if you were getting the same level of recognition, you wouldn't feel envious at all. The real source of your frustration isn't them—it's your own unmet need for approval. That means that lashing out at the other person involved—whether in your mind or in your actions—is nothing more than misplaced frustration. It's like yelling at your kids because you had a bad day at work or picking a fight with someone just because you're in a bad mood. It's unfair to them.

At the root of envy is the desire for approval. That being the case, the real question isn't "Why do they have what I don't?," it's "What can I do to be recognized myself?" Turning your frustration outward is a mistake in thinking.

Look down at your own feet

If you truly want to be acknowledged, focus on what you can control. As mentioned in Chapter 4, this is what the Buddha called *right effort*.

Start by looking inward instead of focusing on the outside world. Reflect on your motivation and what you currently have—your skills, your potential—to kick things off. Your personality, talents and experiences are completely different from those of the person you envy. That means you *can't* expect to achieve success the same way they did. You have a different starting point, a different journey and a different destination.

And yet, we often fixate on those who have already succeeded, thinking if we do what they did, we should get the same results—but that's a trap. Instead of chasing their path, close your eyes and ask, "What is *my* unique way forward?" This means not getting swept away by comparing ourselves to others.

To break free from envy, the first step is to stop looking at the people around you. As discussed in Chapters 1 and 4, all too often we allow ourselves to get caught up in comparison. So, drop the fixation on your presumed rival. Remind yourself that they don't matter. This will help you let go of your anger. Finally, stop holding on to the illusion that you need the same kind of success they have. In this way, you can completely step away from envy.

Then, if you still have the desire to be recognized, ask yourself, "What can I do right now to improve?," "Am I giving my best effort?," "What more can I do?" This shift in thinking will allow you to start focusing on enhancing your own abilities and improving your own work and life. The Zen philosophy of "looking at your own feet" (*kyakka shoko*) is about staying grounded in your own journey. Instead of obsessing over others, look down at where you stand. Take one step at a time, focusing only on what's within your control.

This kind of effort comes naturally, because you only need to focus on yourself and start from wherever you are right now. If you do this, you will find that envy becomes a thing of the past, and that you can humbly enjoy your journey of self-improvement as you move forward.

The Possibility of a Different Role to Play

In the real world, not everyone gets the recognition they want. Unlike air or sunlight, socially valuable things are limited resources. Not everyone can win in the same way. So, what happens if you give things your all, and you still don't get the success you aimed for?

If you stay attached to *being recognized and winning at all costs*, you will remain stuck in a cycle of frustration. That's where envy, insecurity and resentment take root. If your attachment to being recognized fuels your motivation to succeed, then follow it! If it leads to suffering, however, it's a sign that you're approaching your goals from the wrong mindset and it's time to try a new one.

If we start acting from the basic premise of loving-kindness as the Buddha teaches, then we could try asking ourselves, "How can I help someone?" As we've seen, it's all about contributing and being of service to others. Even if the term *loving-kindness* feels like too grand a concept, most people would agree that contributing to another person's life in a meaningful way is fulfilling.

If you are motivated by contribution, your first thought will be, "What role can I play here?" That's where *the life that fits you best* begins.

For so long, we've been chasing the same victories, the same ideas of success. If you're completely satisfied with where you are, that's great. But if you feel even the slightest sense of unease—if something still feels off—then maybe that version of success wasn't meant for you. Maybe it's time to let go of that attachment and rethink the direction you're traveling in.

If you happen to come across someone achieving what you once wanted, don't let envy take over. Instead, shift your perspective. In the spirit of compassion, take a moment to recognize their hard work, acknowledge their efforts and feel genuine respect for what they've accomplished.

If you ever find yourself feeling envy toward someone or a sense of self-doubt, remind yourself of this: "I have a different role to play."

At the end of the day, every human motivation boils down to one thing—contribution. We all just want to be useful. If you can contribute, if you can offer something valuable, no matter how small, if you can wake up each day with a sense of purpose, finding joy in the little moments . . . Isn't that enough?

A Self Untainted by the World

Everyone, to some extent, has faced setbacks and failures. But that doesn't mean you should let your past define you and conclude that you're not good enough. These things occur because each person is born into different circumstances. The environment we're born into, the people we meet, our personalities, abilities and even the timing of our luck—none of these are the same for any two people. The ways our hearts react to various situations is also entirely different because no two people's brains are the same. Since our inner worlds are unique, everything that manifests from them—our words, our actions, our entire lives—will naturally be different, too.

Each person's experience of life is, at its core, incomparable. There is no fair way to measure one person's reality against another's.

Yet, people obsess over their differences—thinking in terms of winners and losers, strengths and weaknesses, or believing others have something they lack. These thoughts are nothing more than unhealthy attachments and delusions. Instead of dwelling on them, it's better to pause, close your eyes and reset.

When you close your eyes, you shut out the overwhelming stimuli that trouble your heart. In that moment, the outside world disappears.

Within this inner space, seek out tranquility and peace. And, beyond that, discover what uniquely brings you joy.

This is how you learn to live *in* the world without being burdened *by* it, free from the pull of every passing impulse.

> *Just as blue, red and white lotuses grow from the depths of the water, rising above its surface without being tainted by it, so too do the enlightened grow and live within this world, yet remain unsoiled by it.*
>
> —**The Connected Discourses**

CHAPTER 6

HAVE A STANDARD FOR THINKING

Returning to the Right Mindset—Again and Again

IF YOU WANT to break free from the restless cycle of dissatisfaction we've discussed in this book and find healing and clarity, you need a new kind of anchor for your heart.

Finding Peace in the Thought "Life Is Enough"

Everyone lives their life doing their best for themselves. No one deliberately sets out to make themselves unhappy or to make mistakes. And yet, no matter how much time passes, that sense of deep contentment—of thinking, "This is enough"—never seems to arrive. Instead, our hearts are always whispering to us that something is still missing. We live in a constant state of thirst.

In truth, the heart is always restless, never fully satisfied. It was the Buddha who first realized its fundamental nature:

> *Everything is burning. The things we see are burning. The mind that sees is burning.*
>
> *Burning with the flames of greed, burning with the flames of anger, burning with the flames of delusion.*
>
> *The heart is ablaze with suffering, decay, loss, sorrow, grief, pain and turmoil.*
>
> —**"Sermon on Gayasisa Hill,"** ***The Connected Discourses***

To say the heart is *burning* means that it is *reacting*. It flares up with desire, anger and delusion. And because of these relentless reactions, people continue to struggle and suffer. As long as the heart keeps reacting, this dissatisfaction—this suffering—will never end.

Perhaps it's time to recognize that this constant thirst, frustration, sadness, anxiety, self-doubt and exhaustion will never be healed unless we cultivate a *new* kind of heart.

This is why we must establish a firm and unwavering anchor within ourselves.

Establishing a True Anchor: *Dhamma*

An anchor is the foundation on which our hearts rely—the philosophy that grounds us. It's something separate from the constantly reacting heart—something we should consciously place before our emotional impulses.

In Buddhism, the path to living correctly, that all people should aspire to, is called *dhamma*—a term that also means truth, law or ultimate reality.

Part of a vow taken by Buddhists, known as "The Threefold Refuge," goes as follows: "I go for refuge to the *dhamma*" ("*Dhammam saranam gacchami*"). To *take refuge* in something means to base your life upon it. It's a promise to live according to the wisdom of the Buddha, the teachings (*dhamma*) and the community of practitioners (*sangha*).

While this might sound like a religious ritual, its essence goes much deeper. *Taking refuge* means making a solemn promise to oneself: "I will anchor my heart in the right way of living." Do you have such an anchor in your heart?

The *right way of living* includes:

1. Understanding reality without reacting impulsively—this is referred to as *right view* in Buddhism.
2. Cleansing the mind of toxic impulses like greed, anger and delusion—a process known as *purification*.
3. Approaching life with the four essential mindsets we explored in the last chapter: *loving-kindness*, *compassion*, *sympathetic joy* and *equanimity*.

This way of living transcends religion. It's an invaluable mindset and a universal guide for all people. You don't have to believe in it or cling to it—it's simply a foundation to place before your reactions, a place of mental stability.

When we anchor our hearts in something solid, we can finally stop drifting through life.

> *A person standing on solid ground in a river is not swept away.*
> *Without firm footing, they are carried off by the current.*
>
> —"In the Garden of Elder Sudatta,"
> *The Connected Discourses*

Rely on Yourself First: A Tough Lesson from the Buddha

Most people seek stability not within themselves, but in the material world—money, possessions, a comfortable lifestyle—or external markers of success, like social status, job titles or education. They believe the answers to happiness lie somewhere *out there*, and if they just work hard enough to obtain them, they will finally feel satisfied.

But what has this constant craving brought us? A never-ending sense of *lack*.

We've seen how human nature is already wired for greed, anger and delusion, and the world stimulates and exploits these tendencies.

If we keep looking to the external world for fulfillment,

we will only end up reacting—caught in a cycle of desire, disappointment and suffering. It's an endless loop of attachment and frustration. Shouldn't we finally recognize this pattern for what it is?

Interestingly, the Buddha himself never encouraged people to depend solely on him or any other external authority. He taught only to rely on oneself and the right way of living. In modern Buddhism, people are often encouraged to seek refuge in the Buddha and the *sangha* (the community of monks and elders), but the Buddha's own teachings were quite different.

In his final days, he gave this advice to his devoted disciple, Ananda:

> *You have no need to rely on anything else.*
>
> *Take only yourself as your anchor, and depend on nothing else in this world.*
>
> *Let the dhamma be your guide—do not cling to the fleeting words or opinions of others.*
>
> —"Encouragement for Ananda,"
> *The Discourse on the Great Passing*

For those desperate to cling on to something, this message may seem daunting. Many seek solace outside themselves because they don't trust their own wisdom—they feel that life is too painful, so they look outward for salvation.

But, as the Buddha tells us, there are no answers in the external world. Everything we encounter—ideologies, beliefs, religions, value systems—is a human construct. They are not *you*. While they might offer temporary comfort, in the end, your inner struggles must be faced by you alone.

That's why we must establish a strong inner foundation—a place of unwavering truth and guidance within ourselves.

This is the Buddha's message.

Step Forward, Step Back, Keep Walking

Maybe right now, you're overwhelmed by endless busyness, exhaustion that won't fade, emptiness, anger, sadness or anxiety. Perhaps you've even found yourself cursing your own life. There may be days when you feel left behind, breathing loneliness.

In moments like these, close your eyes for a while. Feel your breath as it enters and leaves your body. Gaze into the darkness. In that stillness, you will see only one thing—your own heart.

Now, place the right mindset in that heart. For example, embrace a state of awareness dedicated entirely to noticing sensations. Let go of tension, relax and feel your body expanding and contracting. Whisper a wish—"May all living beings be happy." Acknowledge—"Everyone is carrying their own burdens in life."

Return to this mindset again and again. Whenever the

outside world weighs you down, step back into the sacred space within you and reaffirm the right thoughts.

Once you've reclaimed a little bit of yourself, step forward into the world again.

Real life is a cycle of stepping back and moving forward. Returning to the right mindset and choosing to truly live is something you can do as many times as you need, whether it's multiple times a day, for months or even for years.

This practice will lead you to happiness.

Never Lose Sight of the Right Path

The Buddha never wasted time imagining a bleak future. But he also didn't indulge in blind optimism. Instead, he focused on what could be done in the present, wishing with a hopeful heart, "May I reach a good horizon." In essence, his mindset was about trusting in the journey ahead.

Wait, was the Buddha a pessimist?

We often hear terms like *negative thinking* or *pessimism* thrown around. But the truth is, before he awakened to the right way of living, the Buddha himself was deeply troubled by negativity.

Back when he was still just a young man named Gautama—before he became the "Awakened One"—these were the kinds of thoughts that consumed him:

> *All the luxuries of palace life, this healthy body, the youth that people so greatly admire—what do they really mean? The body falls ill, it ages and, eventually, it dies. If everything is bound to be lost in the end, then what is the point of youth, health or even life itself?*
>
> —**"The Suffering of Young Gautama,"** ***The Numerical Discourses***

Gautama was born into royalty and lived a life of extravagant comfort. By most people's standards, he should have had nothing at all to worry about. But, like many of us, he couldn't help but wonder what lay ahead. He realized that everything he enjoyed in his current life would eventually be lost to sickness, aging and death. So, he asked himself, "In that case, what's the point of living?"

We can interpret his struggle in one of two ways. The first perspective is that he was overthinking and being far too pessimistic. The other is that he was sharp—he saw reality exactly as it was—and it was little wonder he later became the Buddha.

In my opinion, both views are correct.

Most people live their lives chasing something they don't yet have. They spend their years pursuing small dreams like material comfort, physical pleasure, the desire for victory or the satisfaction of pride, only to run out of time before they ever feel fulfilled. Some people obsess over what they failed to achieve, carrying regrets, bitterness or resentment until their last breath. Either way, they live at the mercy of an endless desire for *more.*

But Gautama took a different approach. Instead of running on the hamster wheel, he stopped and asked, "No matter how much I gain, in the end, I will lose everything. So, what's the point?"

Call it piercing insight. Call it extreme. Maybe he was just bored of palace life. Maybe he was even dealing with a bout of depression. Whatever the case, feeling "Nothing I do really matters" isn't exactly rare, is it?

What set Gautama apart was what he did next. Instead of sinking into despair, he started searching for a new way to live:

> *People live their lives in pursuit of something. Yet I can't help but think there are two kinds of pursuit: chasing the wrong things and chasing the right things.*
>
> *Chasing the wrong things means longing for the impossible—wishing to stay young forever, to never fall ill, to never face death. But we're all human. Loss is woven into our existence.*
>
> *Chasing the right things begins with seeing this mistake for what it is—searching for a way of life that isn't shackled by suffering, one that rises beyond the fear of loss.*
>
> *And yet, as I stand here now, I realize I have been chasing the wrong things all along.*
>
> —**"The Suffering of Young Gautama,"** ***The Numerical Discourses***

And here, we glimpse the core of what would later become the Buddha's teaching: *right thinking*. One key part of right thinking is choosing the right direction.

Most people spend their lives chasing after youth, health, longevity, wealth, status, recognition and admiration. They orient themselves toward worldly values, believing that acquiring these things will bring them fulfillment.

But the truth is, none of these things are guaranteed. Even if we do manage to grasp them, they won't last. In time, they all slip away. One day, we, too, will be forgotten, as if we had never been here at all.

And yet, we continue to live our lives seeking only to gain and hold on to things.

Gautama looked at this and said, "That is the pursuit of the wrong things. That is a hollow life." To be clear, *freedom from suffering* doesn't mean giving up on life, resigning oneself to despair or rejecting the world. Instead, it means recognizing this: all human beings struggle because life doesn't unfold the way they wish it would. So rather than resisting reality, it's better to seek a way to live no longer bound by suffering.

The Goal—Profound Peace

After years of wrestling with these questions, at the age of 29, Gautama made a bold decision—he would leave behind the world he knew.

Later in life, he reflected on this choice:

> *O seekers of truth, I left home in search of the good.*
>
> —"The Buddha's Later Recollections,"
> *The Discourse on the Great Passing*

Here, the word *good* (*kusala*) refers to a state of deep inner clarity, a mind free from doubt and inner conflict. The young Gautama, after years of struggling with suffering, gave this new direction a name: *the good.*

Ancient scriptures offer us further insight:

> *I will transform this mind that ages and decays into a mind untouched by time.*
>
> *I will transform this suffering heart into stillness, into peace—into the deepest acceptance.*
>
> —"Former Cemetery-Keeper Elder Suppiya,"
> *The Verses of the Elder Monks*

This *deepest acceptance* is the same *good* that young Gautama sought. It refers to a state of mind that is free from suffering.

People are always chasing something—struggling with what they cannot have, tormented by what they have lost. But even within this fleeting world, we can train our minds not to be consumed by it. We can rise beyond suffering and reach a place of profound peace.

Acceptance, like *the good*, is subjective. The moment we can look at our own life and say, "This is enough," we have arrived. And because this peace is a shift in perspective, not in circumstances, it is something we can attain at any stage of life, no matter what situation we find ourselves in.

If we set our direction toward this *acceptance*, all we have to do is keep moving forward, one step at a time. Whether it's our work, our daily responsibilities or our relationships, if we approach them from a place of inner clarity, we will cease to be tossed around by the chaos of the outside world.

Of course, life will never be without struggles. There will always be difficult people and occasions when things don't go our way. But in those moments, instead of reacting impulsively, we can pause—close our eyes, turn inward and return to right thinking. And in doing so, we will hold on to our peace.

No matter how many times we stumble, no matter how painful the journey, we can always begin again—with the goal of one day looking back on our life with satisfaction.

The Buddha's path isn't about changing reality, nor is it about fighting against it. Life will always continue. The world will move forward, with or without us. Struggles will come and go. But the question is—will we add to our own suffering or will we choose a path of peace? What we need is a way of living, thinking and being that allows us to reach our own *deepest acceptance*.

When we take responsibility for this question—"How

should I face this world?"—we discover that we no longer need to escape suffering. We open the door to a way of living that rises beyond it.

> *I did not think rightly. I chased after illusions. I wavered. I wandered. I was led astray by my own desires.*
>
> *But through the Buddha's skillful guidance, I have walked the right path at last. And I am free.*
>
> —"The Confession of the Buddha's Disciple Nanda," *The Verses of the Elder Monks*

Trusting your own life

Finding something to anchor your heart. Seeing the right direction clearly. More than anything else, what matters in life is establishing this path—a way of living that you can trust.

Once you set foot on this path, you will find that your doubts fade away.

You will begin to believe, "As long as I keep walking, I will get there. I will find my peace."

You Can Overcome Any Struggle

The Buddha's message should now be clear to you: every struggle can be overcome. What you need is the right method.

That method refers to how you use your mind. Instead of

reacting blindly and getting caught up in suffering, you train yourself to reset, to see clearly, to adopt a way of thinking that leads to true peace. That has been the central theme of this book.

Buddhism is nothing more than this—a path, a way of living that brings clarity and freedom. Once you stand on this path, you can live your life in reality, occasionally stopping to consider if you're still following the right way to live and, when necessary, step forward anew. There will be moments when your selfish or fearful side resurfaces. You may get swept up in emotions again and pick up new worries along the way. But as long as you remember the path, you will never be truly lost. You can always start over.

When you start living this way, you will begin to see hope in your life. It's when a person stands at the crossroads that they can start to trust in their journey. You will think to yourself, "It's going to be okay. I will definitely get there."

You will get there

Once, there was a nun who came to see the Buddha. She had suffered a tragic past. Though born into a wealthy family, she abandoned them to elope with a servant, only to later lose her husband and both of her children in a single devastating moment. Seeking healing, she threw herself into Buddhist practice, but no matter how hard she tried, her past haunted her. She couldn't break free from her pain.

Then, one day, while washing her feet in a stream, she noticed how the water naturally flowed downward. At that moment, something inside her shifted:

> *I am on the right path.*
> *Just as water flows in one direction, my life, too, will eventually flow beyond suffering.*
>
> —**"The Confession of the Nun Patacara,"** ***The Verses of the Elder Nuns***

She continued practicing and, in time, she was completely freed from her suffering.

When you're struggling, your mind may tell you to blame the past. To resent others. To fear the future. To punish yourself. But none of those will ever provide a real solution.

Instead, remind yourself of this: "I am on the right path. No matter what happens, I will return to this mindset, this way of living." The fact that you can tell yourself this is the best answer.

If you haven't reached that state of certainty yet, then learn. Experiment. Test these teachings for yourself. Find your own anchor—the place inside your heart that you can always return to. Because once you have that, it's only a matter of time.

As long as you focus on living well today, you will get there. You will reach your deepest acceptance.

> *At last, I have climbed out of the water and onto solid ground.*
>
> *The raging currents of my mind once carried me away, but, now, I have reached the path of truth.*
>
> —"The Confession of a Former Non-Believer,"
> *The Verses of the Elder Monks*

Your mind is your sanctuary—one that no external reality can take away from you.

Now, all that remains is what you choose to place inside it.

Cultivate a mindset that will lead you to the deepest acceptance.

Live your life to the fullest.

Stop reacting.

GLOSSARY

adukkhamasukha—a neutral state (see also "*dukkha*" and "*sukha*")

avijja—a mind that simply *doesn't see*; ignorance

Brahmin—the priestly class; highest ranking of the four *varnas* (social classes) in Hindu India

Buddha—the Pali term meaning "one who has achieved total clarity." Often translated as the "Awakened One" (see also "emancipation" and "*vimutti*")

delusion—the state of being caught in unhelpful thought patterns such as overthinking, worrying about the future or dwelling on the past; the everyday fog that keeps us from seeing things as they really are. In Buddhist teaching, it is one of the "Three Poisons" that cause suffering, alongside greed and anger

dhamma—in Buddhism, this is the path to living correctly that all people should aspire to; a term that also means truth, law or ultimate reality

dukkha—the Buddha's term for suffering or unhappiness. It is an ancient Pali term combining the words *du*, meaning "hardship" or "obstruction," and *kha*, which roughly means an "emptiness that cannot be filled"

emancipation—in Buddhist teachings, this is the state reached by the Buddha, who attained the ultimate level of understanding (see "*vimutti*")

fudoshin—the concept of the "immovable mind" in Zen philosophy; a state that cannot be disturbed by anger, doubt, confusion, fear or hesitation

judgment—the practice of making snap decisions about important things, for example, whether you're better or worse than someone else

kusala—a state of deep inner clarity; a mind free from doubt and inner conflict

mana—a Buddhist term that can be translated as ego, pride or arrogance

mindfulness—the modern word for labeling feelings and actions with words; tuning in to your physical sensations (see also "*nen*" and "*sati*")

moha—see "delusion"

nen—the word for mindfulness in the Zen tradition

nibbana—enlightenment; the highest spiritual state. Also called *nirvana*

paticcasamuppada—the Buddhist principle of dependent origination; the basic principle that all things arise depending on other things

samatha—seated meditation; (see "*zazen*")

samu—physical labor done with full mindfulness

sankhara—mental formations; strong emotional energy—feelings, desires, memories or delusions

sati—the word used for mindfulness techniques in the time of the Buddha

sukha—a state of mind of happiness

vipallasa—thinking something exists when it actually doesn't; misbelief. Also called *misapprehension*

vipassana—mindfulness and insight

vimutti—the ultimate level of understanding; the state achieved by the Buddha. Sometimes translated as *liberation* or *release* (see "emancipation")

zazen—seated meditation; (see "*samatha*")